Social Innovation and Entrepreneurship: Case Studies, Practices and Perspectives

Edited by

Dr Brendan Galbraith

and

Professor Francesco Molinari

Social Innovation and Entrepreneurship: Case Studies, Practices and Perspectives

First edition September 2014

Disclaimer: While every effort has been made by the editor, authors and the publishers to ensure that all the material in this book is accurate and correct at the time of going to press, any error made by readers as a result of any of the material, formulae or other information in this book is the sole responsibility of the reader. Readers should be aware that the URLs quoted in the book may change or be damaged by malware between the time of publishing and accessing by readers.

Note to readers.
Some papers have been written by authors who use the American form of spelling and some use the British. These two different approaches have been left unchanged.

Softback ISBN: 978-1-910309-58-2
Hardback ISBN: 978-1-910309-59-9
ePUB ISBN: 978-1-910309-60-5
Kindle ISBN: 978-1-910309-61-2

Printed by Lightning Source

Published by: Academic Publishing International Limited, Reading, RG4 9AY, United Kingdom, info@academic-publishing.org

Available from www.academic-bookshop.com

Contents

About the editors

Dr Brendan Galbraith

Brendan is a senior lecturer in Innovation Management at the Department of Management and Leadership at the University of Ulster. Brendan is a member of the European Network of Living Labs, Business and Management Research Institute, and the Centre for SME Development. Brendan has led EC and national innovation and research projects that are valued at more than £4 million and has published his research in Technovation, R&D Management, International Journal of Operations and Production Management and Technology Analysis and Strategic Management. Brendan has recently founded the Social Enterprise Value Incubator (SEVI). SEVI is a model that embeds social enterprises in research projects, academic enterprise activities and course provision within the Ulster Business School for value creation, appropriation and capture.

Professor Francesco Molinari

Francesco Molinari is an independent research and project manager who has worked for several public and private organizations in Europe, including clients from Belgium, Cyprus, Greece, Israel, Italy, Portugal, Slovenia and the UK. In his career he has been involved in the coordination of (or participation in) about twenty ICT-related R&D and innovation projects at European, national and regional level – many on the topics of eParticipation and eGovernment. For the European Commission, among others, he wrote in 2008 a study for the assessment of the Living Labs approach in the EU innovation and Future Internet scenario. He has done consultancy to several Italian Regions (Piedmont, Apulia, Aosta Valley, Veneto) in topics related to the establishment and management of Living Labs. in 2010-2012 he led a State-Region Working Group aimed at the establishment of PCP (Pre Commercial Procurement) in public administration practice for the Italian Ministry of Economic Development, Department of Cohesion Policy. Currently he is research associate on Frugal Government at Politecnico di Milano and works for the Italian Ministry of Economic Development on a project of technical assistance to the 21 Regions engaged in the design of Smart Specialisation Strategies for the new programming period of Structural Funds (2014-2020). Francesco is also a visiting professor at the Department of Management and Leadership, University of Ulster.

Contributors

Christos Apostolakis, Bournemouth University, UK

Chris Baelus, University of Antwerp, Antwerp, Belgium

Alina Badulescu, University of Oradea, Oradea, Romania

Adriana Borza, University of Oradea, Oradea, Romania

Luísa Carvalho, Setúbal Polytechnic Institute, Portugal

Teresa Costa, Setúbal Polytechnic Institute, Portugal

Ann De Keersmaecker, University of Antwerp, Antwerp, Belgium

Nikolay Dentchev, University of Brussels (VUB) and HUBrussel, Belgium

Cláudia Fernandes, CATIM Technological Centre for the Metal Working Industry, Porto, Portugal

Brendan Galbraith, University of Ulster Business School, Northern Ireland, UK

Jan Jonker, Radboud University Nijmegen (RU), The Netherlands

Prabhu Kandachar, Delft University of Technology, Delft, The Netherlands

Panayiotis Ketikidis South East European Research Centre (SEERC), Thessaloniki, Greece

Francesco Molinari, University of Ulster Business School, Northern Ireland, UK

Panagiotis Parcharidis, CITY College — International Faculty of the University of Sheffield, Thessaloniki, Greece

Vikram Parmar, Delft University of Technology, Delft, The Netherlands

Luís Rocha, CATIM Technological Centre for the Metal Working Industry, Porto, Portugal

Sebastian Sipos-Gug, University of Oradea, Oradea, Romania

Aelita Skaržauskienė, Mykolas Romeris University, Vilnius, Lithuania

Koen Vandenbempt, University of Antwerp, Antwerp, Belgium

The role of the business school in supporting social enterprises: practices and perspectives

Dr Brendan Galbraith and Professor Francesco Molinari,
University of Ulster Business School, Northern Ireland.

In the aftermath of the prolonged economic recession there are renewed efforts amongst policy makers in the UK to expedite further development of the social economy. There is a general sense that the social economy sector, despite the recession, fared reasonably well, and this is a view that was reflected in research across the social economy network and by Government representatives across the UK (DETI, 2011). Sustainability of social innovations and a social economy is paramount in order to develop an environment where society profits and social enterprises excel at meeting community need. In response to this challenge DETI have outlined three strategic objectives for the development of the social enterprise economy, namely:

- Increase awareness of the social economy sector and establish its value to the local economy
- Develop the sector and increase its business strength
- Create a supportive and enabling environment

In a series of responses from stakeholders in the social economy sector there have been calls for research efforts to target national and international networks to identify and source best practice. In addition, leading academic researchers argue that future policies should strive to maintain and develop the distinctive capabilities of third sector organisations and balance between economic, social and environmental objectives (Haugh and Kitson, 2007). These policy and academic conclusions could be interpreted as a rallying call for the research community, particularly business schools, to ramp up their effort to shed light on best practices and triple-bottom line management capabilities and methods.

In this apparent new realism for the social economy, it is important to improve understanding on how to make social enterprises and the social economy itself, more sustainable, and less reliant on public funding. We argue that, an important and, arguably a largely untapped stakeholder are universities. Specifically, what best practices and supportive mechanisms can help to nurture more sustainable social innovations? Progress in this area will not only help cement the social economy into the *'mainstream'* but also help its constituents (social enterprises) move higher up the business value chain, whilst potentially adding value to the universities' *'third mission'* of promoting academic enterprise. From a European perspective, the watchwords when discussing how to improve the social economy are *'social innovation'*. Jose Manuel Durao Barroso, former President of the European Commission is on record as having emphasized this, when he declared: *"I strongly believe that today our strong European tradition of social innovation is more needed than ever."*

In terms of exploiting further innovation adoption in the social economy sector it is imperative to balance the needs of society, appropriate technology and service solutions with sustainable business models. This is an increasingly important challenge for European innovators and constituents of the innovation ecosystem, especially with the complex challenges of national healthcare systems, sustainable energy solutions, social isolation and community cohesion. Moreover, there is enormous untapped potential to extrapolate and upscale successful grassroots social enterprise business models in order to create secondary markets, thus spreading social impact to other communities. We would like to further develop our understanding of the methods and business models that facilitate this, and share best practices and case studies that not only articulate the traditional business logic, but also how these innovations better service the public and benefit society.

As hosts of the 9th European Conference for Innovation and Entrepreneurship 2014 (ECIE 2014), we at the University of Ulster Business School selected the programme theme of *"Societal Driven Innovation and Entrepreneurship"* with the hope to progress this research and practice agenda. To that end ECIE 2014 is a fitting platform to launch the publication of this book. We hope that this book and the ECIE 2014 conference community can help spur more interest into developing better theoretical models of social innovation and social entrepreneurship. As Kurt Lewin's (1952) wise words remind us, *"there is nothing so practical as a good theory"*, and building better theories and models have role to play in guiding public policies, practices and social entrepreneurship education.

1. Understanding social enterprises and the social economy

In the UK the social economy is often referred to as the *'third sector'*, along with the public and private sector, whereas in the US the term *'voluntary'* or *'non-profit'* sector is predominant with the social economy. Moreover, most of what Europeans consider constituents of the social economy has traditionally been virtually excluded from the third sector in US-based research (Lorendahl, 1997). For example, in the US a wide variety of business-type organisations such as mutual insurance companies, savings banks and cooperatives would be considered part of the business sector. Since 1997, the third sector in the UK has received significant government support and has gradually moved from the economic periphery towards the centre, such that it is now instrumental in delivering a range of government policies. It operates alongside the private and public sectors in delivering employment, education, health and social care, housing and environmental policies. The impact of this has been seen in measures of social exclusion, poverty, the environment, social capital, as well as GDP and employment (Haugh and Kitson, 2007).

Moreover, social enterprises typically create jobs for local people, resulting in direct and indirect impacts on the local supply chain and broader economy – all of which is viewed very positively in the current economic environment. For example, the Northern Ireland unemployment rate is at its highest rate for over a decade; and Northern Ireland has the highest economic inactivity rate in the UK – all of which illustrate the challenge in creating employment and where the social economy is viewed to have a key role to play.

Social economy has been an official term in the European Union (EU) since 1989 and the EU definition covers organizational forms, such as cooperatives, mutuals, associations and foundations (Westlund, 2003). However, in the international debate several different concepts have been used interchangeably with social economy, including non-profit sector, not-for-profit sector, solidarity economy, alternative economy and the third system. In the USA, the UK and European countries, non-profit sector and third sector became the most common concept. Among researchers there seems to be a basic, common concordance about the social economy being something between market capitalism and state economy. In the conflict between capitalism and socialism which characterized twentieth century Europe, the social economy became a *'third'* way which was never really dominant but did achieve a sufficiently important position in several Latin countries for it to accorded official EU status (Westlund, 2003). Moreover, a new term has been coined is *'social capitalism'* that seems to sit somewhere between capitalism and socialism, but means different things to different people. For example, Shaughnessy (2012) argues that:

"We don't actually have a strongly delineated sense of what goals this new social capitalism serves. It is defined by collaboration and sharing not by an ideology, unless you talk about the developmental capitalism of Muhammad Yunnis. We don't know how it will impact the economics of capitalism."

Other commentators align social capitalism with the well-established triple bottom line sustainability approach:

"Social capitalists operate with a triple bottom line (TBL) business methodology, which traditionally consists of three "P's": people, planet, profit. TBL's been embraced by many sustainability initiatives as an operational philosophy – educating the public on sustainability and building a community around a cause (people), reducing waste and pollution (planet), and still making some sort of (profit) to help grow and further the cause while supporting those who put effort into it (Nunnery, 2012)."

For many UK policymakers, the social economy offers a means to easing the pressure on the Exchequer and acts only as a bridge between welfare dependency and absorption into the 'mainstream' economy (Amin et al, 1999). For many academic commentators, however the long-term objective of developing the social economy is quite different. Recognising that in those areas hardest hit by deindustrialization and recession the *'mainstream'* economy is unlikely to return in any meaningful way for the foreseeable future, they suggest that the social economy must act as a permanent alternative to the *'mainstream'* economy (Amin et al, 1999).

There are many benefits to the further development of as sustainable social economy. Community-based social enterprises are understood to offer a qualitatively better way of delivering social services and economic regeneration. Community-led social initiatives can provide flexible and cost-effective services directly in response to local need. In addition, where such successful projects take root, they can provide new sources of jobs and contribute positively to the life of the locality (Amin et al, 1999). In particular they are seen as effective in combating social exclusion by actively promoting a 'sense of community' often felt to have been lost in the most deprived areas (Adamson, 1997; Madanipour et al, 1998; Saunders, 1997). And the most daunting challenges such as climate change, ageing and chronic diseases are indeed significant opportunities for social innovation. In order to help target some of these challenges and others, insights from best practices in social innovation and supportive policies would be highly illuminating.

2.   Social Enterprise Value Incubator (SEVI)

To that end the University of Ulster Business School we have recently launched the Social Enterprise Value Incubator (SEVI) as part of the Centre for SME Development.

The Social Enterprise Value Incubator (SEVI) is a knowledge transfer *'incubator'* that aims to add value to social enterprises through their immersion in research projects, academic enterprise activities and innovation and entrepreneurship modules at the Ulster Business School. In this model the *'classroom', 'social enterprise', 'research project'* or *'academic enterprise activity'* will essentially be the *'incubators'* (rather than a traditional incubator building) for social enterprises and provide opportunities to develop value and knowledge transfer opportunities. Moreover, by immersing student project teams in real-world *'living lab'* experiences we hope to develop the awareness, self-efficacy and capacity of students towards social entrepreneurship.

SEVI is a collaborative model and online hub that will adopt several key principles of successful university incubators. Firstly, incubators are not standalone entities and SEVI will follow the exemplar model of those that cleverly interact with and leverage resources from their own regional environments (Autio and Klofsten, 1998). Second, rather than focusing on traditional inputs and outputs measures of success, the activities of SEVI will focus on several dimensions of value: value creation, value appropriation·and value capture. Whereas, many traditional incubators adopt a narrow transaction-based modus operandi, SEVI will work with its local and international ecosystem to cultivate value opportunities for social enterprises (Galbraith et al, 2006). Third, the mission of traditional university incubators has always been known to cause tensions with the established university norms and other strands of core business. However, the activities of SEVI will be completely embedded and synergized in the three core missions of the university: course provision, research and academic enterprises. SEVI will provide opportunities for social enterprises to create and capture value so that they can become sustainable and accelerate their growth (both business and social mission). SEVI will facilitate connectivity with resources, people, networks and opportunities for existing social enterprises and develop the capacity of students and graduates to create new social enterprises.

A key premise of SEVI is that in our engagement with many social enterprises we understand that a significant number of the micro-sized social enterprises, (particularly community development oriented social enterprises) are solely focused on achieving their social mission within their local community, rather than scaling-up and expanding in the same way as, for example, growth-oriented and for-profit SMEs per se. For that reason, there is enormous potential to disseminate successful business models of social enterprises regionally, nationally and internationally to facilitate the creation of secondary markets, especially by harnessing the potential of internet-enabled technology platforms.

We see that the creation of secondary markets across Northern Ireland from successful business models of international social enterprises, and across different regions of Northern Ireland, has the potential to create additionality in the social economy.

To that end SEVI will try to make a contribution by facilitating social enterprises to *'incubate'* their business model (create & capture value) through: (1) inclusion in student cohort consultancy project teams, (2) inclusion in academic enterprise projects and (3) domestic and research projects. In addition to being premised on good practices within the university incubator research literature (Mian, 1996; Autio and Klofsten 1998; Galbraith et al., 2006), SEVI has also been informed by the living lab model (Galbraith and McAdam, 2011). SEVI continues to engage in benchmarking activities within the European Network of Living Labs (ENoLL) and social innovation and enterprise programmes such as *'Emerge'* at Oxford University and *'Innovation Space'* and *'Global Resolve'* at Arizona State University.

In terms of leveraging existing resources within our region, SEVI utilizes existing and complimentary programmes such as the University of Ulster's Science Shop programmes as well as funding schemes that facilitate working with social enterprises including Invest Northern Ireland's Innovation Vouchers, Knowledge Transfer Partnerships and InterTradeIreland's *Fusion* programme. These domestic networks and funding resources are bolstered by a variety of European Commission and international funding instruments that SEVI is fully engaged with. In regard to the latter, there is a wave of technology platforms that promote collective intelligence for social innovation that offer promising potential to scale grass-root sustainability solutions and to share best practices.

At SEVI we have set the following three broad objectives:

1. To develop SEVI into a highly visible gateway for social enterprises to access collaboration opportunities to support their development.

2. To develop the social entrepreneurial awareness and capacity of Ulster Business School graduates

3. To enrich research, course provision and academic enterprise activities that are focused on social innovation and entrepreneurship.

These objectives are underpinned by the following value-based core activities (Table 1).

Table 1: SEVI Core Activities

SEVI CORE ACTIVITIES
• Development of new academic enterprise funded projects that involve or benefit social enterprises
• Development of new research projects involving or benefitting social enterprises
• Development of international linkages to transfer best practices and exemplar case studies of business models of successful social enterprises
• Creation of events, symposia, workshops, master classes that involve and benefit social enterprises
• Development of global student teams for collaborative student project work benefitting social enterprises
• Creation of experiential learning opportunities for students in short-term work placements and work experiences.
• Inclusion of social enterprises in applied assessment activities in innovation and entrepreneurship modules
• Development of a portfolio of case studies of successful social enterprise business models in a variety of sectors from different regions of Northern Ireland and across the world, to provoke their re-use and create secondary markets through growing existing social enterprises or promoting the development of new social enterprises
• Development of a bespoke business model framework and toolkits for social enterprises
• Creation of events, symposia, workshops, master classes that involve and benefit social enterprises
• Delivery of business model development workshops for social enterprises.
• Creation of awareness of the importance of the social economy and social enterprises to both undergraduate and postgraduate students and wider society.
• Creation of a social-entrepreneurs-in-residence programme
• Promotion of the inclusion of guest lecturers, from social enterprises or with relevance to social enterprises, in a variety of modules in the Ulster Business School.

3. Introduction to book

This book was developed to bring together a collection of papers on social entrepreneurship that have been presented at the European Conference for Innovation and Entrepreneurship (ECIE) and International Conference for Innovation and Entrepreneurship (ICIE). The long-running ECIE, now into its 9th year has been a forum to discuss and share case studies, practices and perspectives on social entrepreneurship and in this book we have carefully selected with the potential reader in mind, whether it is an entrepreneurship educator, researcher or practitioner.

We begin the book with a mixed methods study into the attitudes and perceptions of for-profit organisations on social entrepreneurship. After critiquing the social entrepreneurship literature, Ketikidis and Parcharidis conduct their empirical work in Northern Greece. The authors find that although there is implicit awareness and evidence of socially aware practices amongst the for-profit companies, there is also a misconception on how a social enterprise is defined and functions. It is an intriguing *'outside-looking-in'* industrial perspective on social entrepreneurship and an interesting offshoot might be -what would be the key drivers or impediments for some of these for-profit organisations when they consider converting to an explicit social mission, and social enterprise?

We follow with Apostolakis' paper that studies social entrepreneurship from a strategic perspective. Apostolakis elaborates that as *"social entrepreneurship involves individuals and groups that create independent organisations in mobilizing ideas and resources to address social needs"*, and therefore, *"a focus on strategy in this context becomes paramount, as it can give a long-term direction to social enterprises."* Apostolakis' empirical work presents a strategic framework that comprises aspects of mission, decision making power, profit distribution, effectiveness of service delivery and benefits for the local community.

De Keersmaecker et al., then follow with a research a paper that investigates factors that influence an upscaling process of grassroots innovations in India. The authors highlight that *"people within low-income markets have often shown their ability to identify their own problems and generate solutions"*. Therefore, they define 'Grassroots innovations' as "ideas for products and services that respond to the constraint-based context and limited internal resources" - some of which, have been converted from an idea into a business. *"Upscaling a grassroots innovation has the potential to contribute in the regional socio-economic development and if nurtured properly, can be a significant force to empower local communities through inclusive development and job creation".* The key critical factors found in De Keersmaecker et al., findings that influence upscaling grassroots innovation include: the motivation of grassroots innovators; their perception and approach towards upscaling; overcoming isolation in local markets; possibilities for receiving needed support and overcoming institutional formalisations.

Following the papers on attitudes towards social entrepreneurship, strategic approaches that may be adopted and factors that may influence upscaling, we now move to look at the role and potential of social technologies for measuring and managing social impact. In an intriguing paper, Skaržauskienė robustly presents the potential for social technologies to be deployed as a powerful tool for holding organizations accountable for their social impact. Information technology has experienced many cycles of innovation, always producing more complex and integrated sets of technologies to respond directly to societal needs. The paper presents new management practices using social technologies in public administration organizations for addressing complexity, uncertainty and changes. Drawing on qualitative and quantitative evidence the paper is seeking to improve our understanding of the role of social technologies and to give guidance on how to handle the relationship between technologies and entrepreneurship in public administration organizations.

The next four papers that comprise the second half of the book are interrelated, each addressing the important theme of *'sustainability'*.

In their paper, Fernandes and Rocha argue that adopting this principle of sustainability, where the response to actual needs in the present does not compromise the ability of future generations to meet their own needs, should be a pillar in educational systems (either formal or informal) and later on for industrial practices and manufacturing processes. The author's case study research draws on their experiences of utilising an eight-step project approach that focused on experience, innovation and entrepreneurship with young people aged 10-17. The paper contributes an intrinsic pedagogical focus on the process and outputs of this programme and how it can add value to a sustainability approach and product design.

Next, we move to a paper that presents a business model perspective on sustainability. Jonker and Dentchev identify five modelling principles and demonstrate their role and function in an exploratory case study. The authors rightly highlight that most mainstream business model frameworks are corporate-driven and focus exclusively on profit making. To help serve this important gap, they identify five sustainability-related principles that should be addressed in business modelling (in addition to profit-making). This includes: (1) multiple value creation; (2) basic logic; (3) strategic choice; (4) value network and (5) cooperative organizing.

Badulescu et al., explore environmental and support factors of social entrepreneurship. The paper aims to provide information and build knowledge towards a better understanding of the role played by environmental factors in this regard, as well as their perception among young people who intend to be or are involved in Romanian social enterprises. The main practical implication of this research is the need for a change in young individuals' perception on the threats and opportunities that they will face when starting and running a social enterprise. The authors conclude that perception errors inevitably affect their entrepreneurial intent and might prevent valuable individuals from entering the field. Therefore, Badulescu et al., suggest that social entrepreneurship training should also focus on fostering a realistic view of the environmental factors that might impact entrepreneurial success.

The book closes with Costa and Carvalho's research on social enterprise projects listed in a social stock exchange (BVS). BVS replicates the atmosphere of a stock exchange and its role is to approach civil society organizations and social investors that are available to support these organizations by purchasing their social shares. This project is developing innovative approaches to attract financial resources in order to solve social problems, including the eradication of poverty and other social risks. Through the promotion of social investment, the BVS proposes an innovative financial model supported not from a philanthropic or charitable perspective, but according with the social profit of each project. The empirical study is based on interviews with key-informers from social projects included in BVS. The interviews have three main objectives: (1)

identify the degree of project attractiveness; (2) understand the reasons of project attractiveness in terms of funding; (3) assess the sustainability of the projects, concerning economic dimension (e.g. job creation), social dimension (e.g. resolution of a social need for a vulnerable group) and environmental dimension (e.g. reduction of impacts on the environment). The authors suggest that the paper contributes to a better understanding of the factors that promote the attractiveness of social projects and highlight the importance of improvement concerning management practices.

To conclude the main objective of this book is to improve our understanding of social entrepreneurship by investigating management approaches, case study examples and best practices of how social enterprises leverage value for their business model and social mission. We hope that the collection of papers in this book will help stimulate researchers to extend this work and utilise these examples in the classroom. Moreover, we hope that this will help energize academics to build broader links with social enterprises in their core activities as well as help develop the consciousness and capacity of their graduates to engage in social entrepreneurship. We hope you enjoy reading this book and we thank all of the authors for contributing their well-crafted research papers to make this compilation possible.

References

Adamson, D. (1997) 'Communities of resistance: social exclusion, community development and economic regeneration', paper presented to the British Sociological Association Annual Conference, University of York, York 7-10 April.

Amin, A., Cameron, A. and Hudson, R. (1999) 'Welfare at work? The potential of the UK social economy'. Environment and Planning. 31 pp 2033-2051.

Autio, E. and Klofsten, M. (1998) A comparative study of two European business incubators. Journal of Small Business Management. 36 1 pp 30-43.

DETI (2011) 'Department of Enterprise, Trade and Investment Social Economy Evaluation Assignment'. KPMG. July.

Galbraith, Brendan and McAdam, Rodney (2011) The promise and problem with open innovation. Technology Analysis & Strategic Management, 23 (1). pp. 1-6.

Galbraith, B., McAdam, R. and Humphreys, P. (2006) A Tri-national study of business support services in Science and Technology Parks (STP). In:

XXIII IASP World Conference on Science and Technology Parks 2006, Helsinki, IASP.

Haugh, H. and Kitson, M. (2007) 'The Third Way and the third sector: New Labour's economic policy and the social economy'. Cambridge Journal of Economics, 31 pp 973-994.

Lee, R. (1995) 'Look after the pounds and the people will look after themselves: social reproduction, regulation, and social exclusion in Western Europe'. Environment and Planning. 27 pp 1577-1594.

Lewin, K. (1952). Field theory in social science: Selected theoretical papers by Kurt Lewin. London: Tavistock.

Lofsten, H. and Lindelof, P. (2002) Science Parks and the growth of new technology-based firms – academic-industry links, innovation and markets. Research Policy. 31 pp 859-876.

Lorendahl, B. (1997) 'Integrating the public and cooperative/social economy towards a new Swedish model'. Annals of Public and Cooperative Economics. 68 3 pp379-395.

Madanipour, A., Cars, G. and Allen, J. (Eds.) (1998) 'Social Exclusion in European Cities: Processes, experiences and responses'. (Jessica Kingsley, London).

Mian, S. A. (1996) Assessing value-added contributions of university technology business incubators to tenant firms. Research Policy. 25 pp 325-335.

Nunnery, B. (2012) We are Social Capitalists. 14th June. Available from: http://in.gredients.com/2012/06/14/were-social-capitalists/

Saunders, R. (1997) 'Resident Services Organisations. Priority Estates Project'. 2 Albert Mews, Albert Street, London N4 3RD

Shaughnessy, H. (2012) The emergence of Social Capitalism: Adaptation or Threat? Forbes. 23rd January. Available at: http://www.forbes.com/sites/haydnshaughnessy/2012/01/23/the-emergence-of-social-capitalism-adaptation-or-threat/

Westlund, H. (2003) 'Form or contents? On the concept of social economy'. International Journal of Social Economics. 30 11/12 pp 1192-1206

Conceptions and Attitudes towards Social Entrepreneurship and Social Enterprises: The Case of Northern Greek For-Profit Companies

Panayiotis Ketikidis[1, 2] and Panagiotis Parcharidis[1]
[1]CITY College – International Faculty of the University of Sheffield, Thessaloniki, Greece
[2]South East European Research Centre (SEERC), Thessaloniki, Greece

Abstract: An effort to define the context of social entrepreneurship and social enterprises in the northern Greek for-profit business field has inspired and directed this research. Social entrepreneurship and social enterprises are issues that present high academic interest, and are still in developing stage. This study seeks to outline the context of this important field of research, and to explore the conceptualisation and the attitude of Northern Greek for-profit companies towards social entrepreneurship and social enterprise practices. A literature review is presented covering themes relevant to social entrepreneurship and social enterprises, and provides the background to the research design, which combines quantitative and qualitative methodology in order to achieve the study's objectives. In the context of the quantitative approach, a web-based survey with the participation of 72 northern Greek for-profit companies was carried out, and following descriptive data analysis, indicators of social entrepreneurship practices and concepts were examined. In the context of the qualitative approach, 10 interviews with key managers of northern Greek for-profit companies were conducted in order to investigate attitudes towards the themes in question. The results suggest that northern Greek for-profit companies seem to be socially oriented, and managers tend to welcome social entrepreneurship practices. There are misperceptions of the terms, and social enterprises seem to be perceived as non-profit organisations. Despite the fact that there were valuable and interesting findings, the conduct of the web-based survey limited the sample size, presenting a low response rate, and an in-depth statistical analysis of relationships and correlations was not executed. This study is a first step in examining social entrepreneurship in Northern Greece and it contributes to the enrichment of knowledge of the researched field.
Keywords: social entrepreneurship, social enterprises, northern Greece, for-profit companies

1. Introduction

During the last two decades, there has been a rising academic interest in examining social entrepreneurship and social enterprises. In fact, several authors have provided different theoretical directions concerning social entrepreneurship (Austin et al, 2006; Hartigan, 2006; Korosec and Berman 2006; Mair and Marti, 2006; Peredo and McLean, 2006; Drayton, 2002; Dees, 2001) and social enterprises (Haugh, 2005; Roper and Cheney, 2005; Harding, 2004; Dees, 1998). Each of them has examined different traits of the researched terms in order to contribute to the development of a general framework. Despite a recent focus on social enterprises and social entrepreneurship, the topic presents research gaps and controversial issues. Several aspects of social entrepreneurship can be identified (Martin and Osberg, 2007; Hartigan, 2006; Korosec and Berman; 2006; Mair and Marti, 2006; Nicholls 2006; Peredo and McLean, 2006; Pomerantz 2003; Roberts and Woods, 2005; Drayton, 2002; Dees, 2001); many authors discuss different types of social enterprises, as they belong to a sector where many forms of these organisations can be identified. According to Zahra et al., despite of the increasing academic interest in social economy and social entrepreneurship, there is no common conceptual agreement and understanding of these concepts (Zahra et al, 2009).

The main objective of this paper is to explore the conceptualisation and the attitude of Northern Greek for-profit companies towards social entrepreneurship and social enterprises' practices. The following sections briefly outline concepts about social entrepreneurship; provide insights into social enterprises; present possible links between the researched terms and corporate social responsibility; show the benefits, the barriers and the limitations of social entrepreneurship and social enterprises; and examine three case examples in order to clarify the researched issues. Finally, a section dedicated to the methodology, with an interpretation of the data gathered, and concluding remarks concerning social entrepreneurship and social enterprises.

2. The landscape of social entrepreneurship and social enterprises

Although its beginnings go back to the 1980s, literature related to social entrepreneurship and social entrepreneurs started conceptualising these terms in the late 1990s and the beginnings of the 2000s. It should be recognised that the particular research field has been benefited from the previous work on the term entrepreneurship (Austin et al, 2006; Mair and Marti, 2006) (Figure 1). Alertness (Tang, 2009; Anderson, 2005; Kirzner, 2009, 1997), risk-taking (Brouwer, 2000, 2002), innovation (Langlois, 2007; Brouwer 2002) and creativity (Wennekers and Thurik, 1999) are traits that dominate entrepreneurship, and they are also applicable to social entrepreneurship. Indeed, several authors have employed characteristics of traditional entrepreneurship in order to develop the dimensions of the term social entrepreneurship. These dimensions are provided as it follows, and social entrepreneurship can be considered as:

- The creation of social value through innovation, risk-taking, and the recognition and exploitation of opportunities for the improvement of society (Hartigan 2006; Peredo and McLean, 2006; Weerawardena and Mort, 2006);

- A multidimensional collaboration between profit-seeking ventures, non-profit organisations and community organisations, directed towards social improvement (Korosec and Berman 2006; Mair and Marti, 2006; Roper and Cheney, 2005; Pomerantz, 2003);

- Actions of one or more individuals with the goal to ameliorate society through collaboration between the public, private and not-for-profit sectors (Roper and Cheney, 2005) (Figure 1).

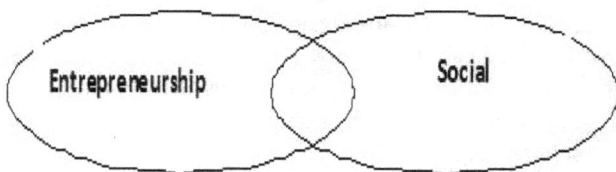

Figure 1: Link between entrepreneurship and social entrepreneurship

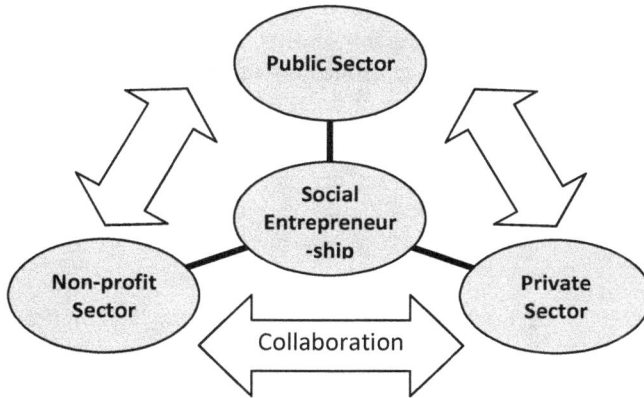

Figure 2: Forms of social entrepreneurship

Social Entrepreneurs are conceptualised as:

- Individuals who spot problematic aspects of society, trying to resolve them, creating better social conditions (Drayton, 2002);

- Individuals who enter the business world with social impact as their primary motive (Roper and Cheney, 2005; Prabhu, 1999);

- A means for an investment to be transformed into social good (Weerawardena and Mort, 2006);

- Young and altruistic individuals, compelled to fight injustice (Prabhu, 1999);

- Innovative directors who are socially responsible, administrators of non-profit organisations and philanthropists (Roper and Cheney, 2005).

2.1. Insights of social enterprises

The realisation of entrepreneurial concepts in the social sphere follows the theoretical foundation of social entrepreneurship. Social enterprises are the enactment of the above (Figure 2), and they are ventures that are created by social entrepreneurs (Haugh, 2005). In particular, social enterprises can be understood as:

- Innovative ventures in the social sphere, with different structure, strategy and norms from the non-profits, responding to socio-political changes and problems, and producing valued results for the society through their programs (Korosec and Berman, 2006; Dart, 2004);

- Enterprises with social ends (primary goal) which generate revenues (secondary goal) from their activity, like mainstream businesses, and they reinvest them internally so as to grow as firms, reaching more people in need (Hartigan, 2006; Harding, 2004; Lingane and Olsen. 2004);

   Ventures in the private, public and not-for-profit sector (Roper and Cheney, 2005): *In the private as ventures who have social impact through their trading activities (pure social enterprises);*

   In the public as a collaboration between community organisations with profit-seeking corporations; and

   In the not-for-profit sector as non-profit organisations with the structure and the mentality of traditional businesses, operating with donations and grants;

- An alternative way of thinking beyond financial transactions, broadening the individualistic conceptualisation of the traditional profits (Ridley-Duff, 2007).

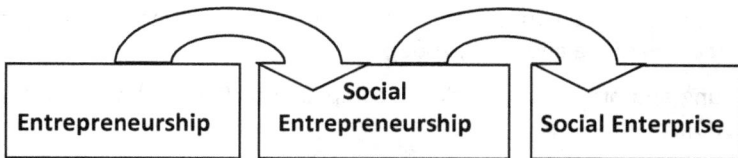

Figure 3: Evolution of social enterprise

Overall, pure social enterprises are placed between the philanthropic or non-profit organisations and the traditional or commercial businesses. A pure social enterprise combines the traits of the above extremes (Figure 4). Social enterprises are characterised by mixed motives, benevolence on the one hand and self-interest on the other. They deal with a double bottom line; social ends and profit motives (Dees, 1998). That is to say, the method that they follow is balanced between their social mission and the market drivers (Mort et al, 2003). They differentiate from the conventional businesses, given that they reinvest their surpluses in the business or in the community, and they do not seek to maximise profits for the shareholders or the owners. Their goal is to provide social and economic value; the first for alleviating social problems and the second for expanding, meeting and satisfying social needs as far as possible. In relation to capital, social enterprises combine the donations and grants with the revenues from their operations in order to function. Since they are in between non-profits and traditional firms, their workforce, which is limited (Vidal, 2005), can consist of volunteers or fully paid staff, who can benefit from tax provisions by the state or discounts from suppliers.

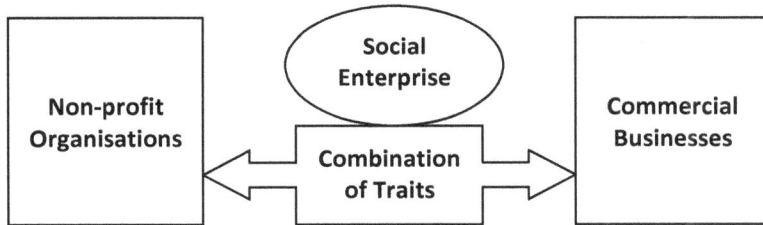

Figure 4: Position of a social enterprise

Table 1 presents the taxonomy of the academic articles that particularly aimed at the term social enterprise.

Table 1: Taxonomy of the literature on social enterprises

Author (Year)/ Methodology	Theme	Issues	Critique/ Comment
Cannon (2000)/ Literature review and cases studies of the public sector	Community organisations and social entrepreneurs	Mainstream business should get more initiatives in order for the public sector to be more effective	
Catford (1998)/ Literature review	Traits of social entrepreneurs	Social entrepreneurs need supportive environments in order to operate	
Cornelius et al (2008)/ Literature review	Social enterprises and corporate social responsibility	Identification of markers that measure corporate social responsibility practices	Community organisations based corporate social responsibility activities are often well developed in private sector
Dart (2004)/ Literature review	Institutional perspectives of social	Moral legitimacy is connected with the	Social enterprises are understood in

Author (Year)/ Methodology	Theme	Issues	Critique/ Comment
	enterprises	emergence of social enterprises	more narrow and revenue-generation terms
Dees (1998)/ Case examples	The need to commercialise non-profit organisations	Options for non-profit organisations in order to be more effective	Need for innovation in the social sector
Defourny and Nyssens (2008)/ Literature review and presentation of social enterprises data in European countries	Different types of social enterprises	Trends and future developments in European countries	The meaning of social enterprise varies between the European countries
Harding (2004)/ Case studies of the UK	Social enterprises play an important role in the provision for economical and social needs	The meaning of social enterprise remains a matter of debate	The key traits of social enterprises are their social aims and social ownership in combination with the generation of profits
Henton et al (1997)/ Case studies of the US	Civic entrepreneurship and communities	Characteristics and leadership roles of the civic entrepreneurs	Nowadays, communities need to collaborate with civic entrepreneurs in order to compete
Kerlin (2006)/ Literature review between European and American theories	Synopsis of definitions of social enterprises between European and American academics and practitioners	Historical factors, institutional and legal environments shaped the conceptualisation of social enterprise	Both regions can learn from the experience of the other in relation with social enterprises
Lingane and Olsen (2004)/ Analysis of studies on entrepreneurs	Measurement of the enterprises' social return on investment	Guidelines for measurement	

Author (Year)/ Methodology	Theme	Issues	Critique/ Comment
Moore et al (2009)/ Literature review and exploratory study in the UK	Criteria for responsible practices	The majority of the criteria are applicable in the UK	Further research is needed in the field
Mort et al (2003)/ Literature review	The need for introduction of new social enterprises and the improvement of the existing ones	Social entrepreneurship as a multidimensional model	
Ridley-Duff (2007)/ Literature review	A framework for social enterprises proposed by individualistic and communitarian philosophy	Social enterprises have adopted other approaches so as to deal with the social exclusion	The framework offers a way to understand the diversity of the field
Tracey et al (2005)/ Literature review	Community organisations and corporate social responsibility	Traits of the community organisations	
Vidal (2005)/ Literature review and report for the Spanish case of work integration	The work-integration in social enterprises	Work-integration social enterprises aim to help individuals who are socially excluded to return to the labour market	

2.2. Barriers and limitations about social entrepreneurship and social enterprises

Due to the fact that social entrepreneurship and social enterprises are modern and in a developing stage, terms may lead to misperceptions. As a new field, more research is needed in order for asocial entrepreneurship theory to be devised (Nicholls, 2006). Particularly, the main barriers and limitations that these modern terms face are:

- The indiscrimination between social enterprises, non-profit organisations and mainstream businesses, since their primary aim is closely connected (Martin and Osberg, 2007);

- The confusion between social enterprises and mainstream businesses that employ socially responsible practices (Cornelius et al, 2008; Defourny and Nyssens, 2008);

- The different understanding of their meaning and the distinctive forms of social enterprises between the US and Europe, and between the different European countries (Defourny and Nyssens, 2008; Kerlin, 2006);

- The practical implications of to operating in a market-driven environment, on the one hand, with which mainstream businesses are familiar. On the other hand, the public resistance in order to raise funds, achieving donations or gain political advantages.

2.3. Case examples

A reflection on the concepts surrounding social entrepreneurship and social enterprises is provided in this section. Three case examples are presented briefly in order for the practical aspects of the researched terms to be considered.

2.3.1. Grameen Bank

Grameen Bank is a microfinance institute that reflects the vision of its founder. Dr. Yunus has been aiming to eliminate poverty in the world and launched this social enterprise that is based on the following dimensions:

- Loan offers to those who have extremely low income and especially to marginalised people (Haque and Harbin, 2009; Yunus, 2007; Kobeissi, N. and Damanpour, 2003; Schicks, 2007). Its lending policy is easily accessible to the borrowers since it does not require collateral (Haque and Harbin, 2009);

- Lending under the premise that the borrower will use the credit to develop his/ her business and create work opportunities, since credit is viewed as a weapon against poverty and unemployment. Indeed five per cent (5 %) %) of the bank members move out of poverty on a yearly basis (Yunus, 2007);

- Scholarship programs and healthcare for all the bank members, to improve their living conditions (Yunus, 2007);

- Collaboration between the institution and the borrowers in order for the latter to be able to repay the loans or to improve the outcome of their work (Haque and Harbin, 2009; Kobeissi, N. and Damanpour, 2003);

- A special business model based on a shareholder scheme where the client is part of the ownership team, affecting the way the bank operates. That is to say, repayments are simultaneously credits for other clients (Schicks, 2007).

2.3.2. The Fifteen Restaurant

Fifteen is one of the most popular United Kingdom's social enterprises (www.socialenterprise.org.uk). It was launched by the famous chef Jamie Oliver in 2002 and it operates with four (4) stores according to the following criteria:

- Providing help with training programs for disadvantaged people from 16 to 24-years-old that would like to become chefs. The majority of Fifteen's employees have criminal backgrounds or have suffered from addictions or homelessness and have the desire to work on the food industry (www.socialenterprise.org.uk);

- Aiming to raise awareness of the importance of nutritious food. It serves food of the highest quality made from the best ingredients (www.fifteen.net);

- A business model that is based on the profit generation and hiring policies of a conventional restaurant; it offers employment opportunities to special populations whose desire is to work in the food industry (www.jamieoliver.com).

2.3.3. The Body Shop

Body Shop is a manufacturer and retailer of natural biodegradable cosmetics. It was founded by Annita Roddick and combines the profit values with the social ones (Hartman and Beck-Dudley, 1999). The company's philosophy is based on the founder's ambitions to produce natural cosmetics and through their trading to have an impact on society and the environment. As a business, it follows the socially responsible practices path. The following provide a clearer picture of Body Shop:

- An environment based on such values as trust and respect is promoted among its stakeholders through its innovative hiring practices and employees' training programs. Consumers purchase responsible sourced products that the trained and informed employees sell (Sillanpaa, 1998);

- The company supports social and environmental develop as it organises and participates in many campaigns for the protection of the environment (www.thebodyshop.com) and collaborates with many non-profit organisations to improve the life of the marginalised people (Roy and Ghosh, 2008);

- The business model is characterised by the profit generation through sales and social and environmental policies, along with the production of environmental-friendly cosmetics and promotion of their other social concerns.

Table 2: Comparison of key traits of social entrepreneurship and social enterprises with case examples

Traits of Social Entrepreneurship and Social Enterprises	Case Examples		
	Grameen Bank	Fifteen Restaurant	The Body Shop
Partnership with Profit-Seeking Organisations (Pomerantz, 2003)	✓	✓	
Meet Needs of Special Populations (Korosec and Berman, 2006)	✓	✓	
Social Impact through Trading Activities (Roper and Cheney, 2005)	✓	✓	✓
Collaboration with Non-Profit Organisations (Tracey et al, 2005)	✓		✓
Reinvestment of Profits (Harding 2004)	✓	✓	
Social Ends and Profit Generation (Dees, 1998)	✓	✓	

3. Analysis and discussion of key findings

3.1. Methodology

This paper explores the conceptualisation of social entrepreneurship and social enterprises, and the attitudes of Northern Greek mainstream businesses towards social entrepreneurship and social enterprises concepts and practices. A combined quantitative and qualitative approach was employed in order to reach to a much deeper understanding of the issues in question (Hohental, 2006). A quantitative approach allowed the statistical analysis of the collected data (Saunders et al, 2007), whilst a qualitative approach was used to describe special phenomena and produce data that were rich in detail (Lasch and Yami, 2008).

The findings of the literature influenced the design of an online questionnaire. The participants in this survey were required to report their understanding of social entrepreneurship and social enterprises' policies and practices. They were further asked about concepts that reflect social oriented behaviors. Finally, they were required to report their comprehension of the researched terms.

Moreover, the sample that participated was purposive, selecting 800 companies operating in Northern Greece. This non-probability sample is considered justifiable, since it most likely covers most of the active companies that operate in different cities of Northern Greece and in distinctive fields. A web based administration of the questionnaire was undertaken, since it was a fast, flexible and cost-saving procedure (Kwak and Radler, 2002; Cook et al, 2000).72 companies participated. The results were subject to descriptive data analysis in order to demonstrate indicators of the issues in question.

Conducting interviews was a tool that provided more qualitative information, along with more depth, representation and value (Palmerino, 1999). Interviewees were asked about their beliefs regarding current managers and their companies, non-profit organisations, social practices and private initiatives, social enterprises' concepts, and the obstacles and challenges of social entrepreneurship in the Greek context. Issues that identified in the literature review influenced the designing of the interview questions. Dees' approach (1998, 2001) to social entrepreneurship and social enterprises guided the qualitative approach. Thus, semi-structured interviews were realised so as to understand the meaning that the interviewees gave to the present research topic (Saunders et al., 2007).

Furthermore, the research was based on a convenience sampling, and 10 qualitative, semi-structured interviews with managers from different fields were conducted. Their companies operate in Thessaloniki but, their activities have impact in Northern Greece. Finally, the data collected was analysed and findings were interpreted through content analysis.

3.2. Indicators towards social entrepreneurship and social enterprises practices

The online survey has demonstrated that, although the majority of the respondents are motivated by salary or the generation of profits, there was a tendency toward social contribution as a work motive. Social enterprises are placed between non-profit organisations and conventional businesses, with social contribution as a primary mission (Dees, 1998). The traditional companies examined are motivated by growth and profit generation, given that they are for-profit companies. Moreover, the majority of the companies neither donates nor collaborates with non-for profit organisations. It is notable that there is a significant percentage of social orientation among the respondents' answers.

Furthermore, there are three categories of social entrepreneurs who want to reach more people in need; managers of mainstream businesses with social responsible practices, managers of non-profit organisations and philanthropists (Roper and Cheney, 2005). The vast majority of respondents are managers of mainstream businesses, while the other two categories are of equal prominence. Additionally, social enterprises reinvest their profit or dividend in order to grow and satisfy their social goals (Hartigan, 2006; Harding, 2004; Dees, 1998). A great portion of the responses of the online survey reveal that the profits or dividends of the examined companies are used by the owners, while they tend to consider the above policy of social enterprises as important. Furthermore, social enterprises' workforce can comprise of volunteers (Vidal, 2005; Dees, 1998) and marginalised people (Fifteen Restaurant). Respondents tend to consider the volunteer work to be important, while they are less sure about the importance of hiring marginalised people.

In addition, on one hand, respondents believe that cooperatives or community organisations and non-profit organisations tend to be more important than businesses in terms of their contribution to the society. On the other hand, the responses demonstrate that businesses tend to contribute more to the economy of a country than cooperatives or community organisations and non-profit organisations. Also, responses of the survey demonstrate that, cooperatives or community organisations and non-profit organisations best satisfy the needs of special populations;

cooperatives or community organisations best correspond to governmental reductions or to the incapability of the local authorities.

Overall, responses reflect that non-profit organisations or community organisations function better towards social purposes, while businesses function better towards economic ends. Since in the Greek context there is no official definition of the term social enterprise (Ziomas et al, 2001, in Borzaga and Defourny (eds), 2004), it could be said that, a venture that employs traits of the two extremes, for-profits and non-profits (Dees, 1998), could operate, with social and economical ends. However, the majority of the respondents tend to consider a social enterprise as a socially oriented organisation, describing it as a non-profit organisation or a community organisation, with a few considering it to be a business.

3.3.   Attitudes towards social entrepreneurship and social enterprises

Interviewees reveal that the basic job motive is the salary in order for the individuals to satisfy their material needs. However, they mention that social contribution can be additional job motive for the current managers. In the context of the companies' mission they argue that their main purpose is to generate profits. Social recognition and creating better conditions of life through their products or services, are mentioned as other companies' missions. Furthermore, interviewees state that, non-profit organisations and community organisations are important. Each of these might face operational problems and obstacles, or be misunderstood in the context of the extent to which they are indeed non-profit. A possible collaboration between businesses and non-profit organisations is considered as necessary by the interviewed managers, to resolve problems in the operation of the State or non-profit organisations. However, they mention that the above can be realised only by companies that they have secured their operational costs or in general by big companies, and that, in such collaborations there is lack of communication.

In the context of social corporate responsibility, interviewees reveal that it is an important social practice in order for conventional businesses to contribute to society. Though, due to the current difficult financial situation, such policies could not be employed by small companies. Also, many interviewees refer to companies with corporate social responsibility as social enterprises. In addition, the managers welcome the hiring policies of social enterprises, even though none of them have employed marginalised people, provided that the possible employee fulfils the requirements of the job.. Also, the majority of the interviewees accept the value of volunteer work, and many of them have implemented it in their operations in the form of student internships. However, some of them believe that volunteer work cannot be applied to for-profit companies.

Furthermore, interviewees state that all the entrepreneurial traits (innovation, creativity, risk-taking and alertness) are necessary so as to identify and exploit an opportunity. In the context of private initiatives towards the social sphere, they claim that, since there is a gap they can fill it. They consider these initiatives to be as important and they mention that, they can be realised as joint ventures between companies or as collaboration with the State. Though, managers state that, companies cannot substitute the role of the State. Finally, interviewees welcome organisations with double bottom lines (profit generation and social ends). They state that these ends should be supplementary. Although the double bottom line could be an ideal scenario, a company that has social ends could generate more profits. However, it is believed that for-profit companies have an indirect social purpose, through the payment of taxes to the State, which in turn will redistribute them through its social policies.

3.4. Research limitations

Generally, the main limitations of this paper are associated with the potential subjectivity of participants' responses, due to the understanding of the questions, and due to the introduction and translation across languages of relatively new terms, despite the efforts to mitigate this risk by providing explanations of the subject. In the context of the quantitative element, the study was limited by the sample size, since generally, web-based surveys have a low response rate (Cook et al, 2000). Also, the nature of the field, which mainly focuses on the generation of theory and literature reviews, led the paper to be more based on concepts of the literature in order to design the web-questionnaire. Therefore, a more in-depth statistical analysis of relationships and correlations was not feasible for by this study.

4. Conclusions and recommendations for further research

The topic of social entrepreneurship and social enterprises has emerged as a response to the economic, technological, political and demographic changes of the three last decades (Henton et al, 1997). Greece stands far behind in the execution and definition of these terms, and little research has been done in the Greek academic field (Defourny and Nyssens, 2008; Ziomas et al, 2001, in Borzaga and Defourny, 2004). This paper is a first step in examining social entrepreneurship in Northern Greece, contributing to the general knowledge of the field.

The findings have demonstrated that Northern Greek for-profit companies seem to be positively inclined to social orientation, though interviews have revealed that problems may emerge in this direction. Also, there are indicators of social entrepreneurship and social enterprises among conventional businesses in Northern Greece, with managers' attitudes tending to welcome such practices. Additionally, the conceptualisation of social enterprises tends to the non-profit organisations side for the respondents to the questionnaire although interviewees seem to comprehend social enterprises; there are misperceptions of the researched terms. Overall, the interviewees' attitude towards social enterprises as a venture tends to be positive, and challenging as an activity in Northern Greece since various obstacles may occur in the Greek context. The findings of this study reflect the tendencies and attitudes of the Northern Greek for-profit companies towards social entrepreneurship and social enterprises. It may therefore be suggested that similar studies should be conducted in other Greek regions in order to examine the general Greek behavior towards the researched subject. Also, it would be interesting to carry out similar studies in specific sectors of the Greek industry in order to examine how the traits of social entrepreneurship are evaluated and comprehended by each of them.

Future research should investigate and explore the conceptualisation of social entrepreneurship by non-profit or community organisations. It may be feasible to come to conclusions about a framework of social enterprises in both the view of non-profits and for-profits. In general, future research should develop a more specific definitions for social entrepreneurship and social enterprises. This would strengthen the theoretical foundations on which researchers can stand, in order to carry out more advanced studies about these terms.

References

Anderson, D., E. (2005) "The spatial nature of entrepreneurship", *The Quarterly Journal of Austrian Economics"*, Vol. 8, No. (2), pp. 21-34.

Austin, J., Stevenson, H. and Wei-Skillern, J. (2006) "Social and commercial Entrepreneurship: Same, different or both?", *Entrepreneurship Theory and Practice*, Vol. 30, No. 1, pp. 1-22.

Borzaga, C. and Defourny, J. (2004) *The Emergence of Social Enterprise*, Routledge, London.

Brouwer, M. (2000) "Entrepreneurship and uncertainty: Innovation and competition among the many", *Small Business Economics*, Vol. 15, No. 2, pp. 149-160.

Brouwer, M., T. (2002) "Weber, Schumpeter and Knight on entrepreneurship and economic development.", *Journal of Evolutionary Economics*, Vol. 12, No.1/2, pp. 83 – 105.

Cook, C., Heat, F. and Thompson, R., L. (2000) "A meta-analysis of response rates in web-or-Internet based surveys.", *Educational and Psychological measurement*, Vol. 60, pp. 821-826.

Cornelius, N., Janjuha-Jivraj, S., Woods, A. and Wallace, J. (2008) "Corporate Social Responsibility and the social enterprise.", Journal *of Business Ethics*, Vol. 81, No. 2, pp. 355-370.

Dart, R. (2004) "The legitimacy of social enterprise.", *Nonprofit Management and Leadership*, Vol. 14, No. 4, pp. 411 – 424.

Dees, G., J. (1998) "Enterprising nonprofits.", *Harvard Business Review*, Vol. 76, No. 1, pp. 55-67.

Dees, G., J. (2001) "The meaning of social entrepreneurship.", *Stanford Business School*, pp. 1-5.

Defourny, J. and Nyssens, M. (2008) "Social enterprise in Europe: Recent trends and developments.", *Social Enterprise Journal*, Vol. 4, No.3, pp. 202-228.

Drayton, W. (2002) "The citizen sector: Becoming entrepreneurial and competitive as business.", *California Management Review*, Vol. 44, No. 3, pp. 120-132.

Fifteen Restaurant. *Fifteen's mission.* [online]. Available from: http://www.fifteen.net/mission/Pages/default.aspx [accessed on 27/07/2010].

Haque, M., A. and Harbin, J., L. (2009) "Microcredit: A different approach to traditional banking: empowering the poor.", *Academy of Banking Studies Journal*, Vol. 8, No. 1, pp. 1-13.

Harding, R. (2004) "Social enterprise: The new economic engine.", *Business Strategy Review*, Vol. 15, No. 4, pp. 39 – 43.

Hartigan, P. (2006) "It's about people, not profits.", *Business Strategy Review*, Vol. 17, No. 4, pp. 42-45.

Hartman, C., L. and Beck-Dudley, C., L. (1999) "Marketing strategies and the search for virtue: A case analysis of the Body Shop.", *International Journal of Business Ethics*, Vol. 20, No. 3, pp. 249-263.

Haugh, H. (2005) "A research agenda for social entrepreneurship." *Social Enterprise Journal*, Vol. 1, No. 1, pp. 1-12.

Henton, D., Melville, J. and Walesh, K. (1997) "The age of civic entrepreneur: Restoring civic society and building economic community.", *National Civic Review*, Vol. 86, No. 2, pp. 149-156.

Hohental, J. (2006) "Integrating qualitative and quantitative methods in research on international entrepreneurship.", *Journal of International Entrepreneurship*, Vol. 4, No. 4, pp. 175-190.

Jamie Oliver. *Fifteen Restaurant*. [online]. Available from:http://www.jamieoliver.com/fifteen [accessed on 27/07/2010].

Kerlin, J., A. (2006) "Social enterprise in the United States and Europe: Understanding and learning from the differences.", *Voluntas: International Journal of Voluntary and Nonprofit Organizations*, Vol. 17, No. 3, pp. 246-262.

Kirzner, I., M. (1997) "Entrepreneurial discovery and the competitive market process: An Austrian approach.", *Journal of Economic Literature*, Vol. 35, No. 1, pp. 60-85.

Kirzner, I., M. (2009) "The alert and creative entrepreneur: A clarification",. *Small Business Economics*, Vol. 32, No. 2, pp. 145-152.

Kobeissi, N. and Damanpour, F. (2003) "From poor to entrepreneur: An innovative strategy to entrepreneurship and small business development.", *Journal of Enterprising Culture*, Vol. 11, No. 4, pp. 399-405.

Korosec, R., L. and Berman, E., M. (2006) "Municipal support for social entrepreneurship." *Public Administration Review*, Vol.66, No. 3, pp. 448 – 462.

Kwak, N. and Radler, B. (2002) "A comparison between mail and web surveys: Response pattern, respondent profile, and data quality.", *Journal of Official Statistics*, Vol. 18, No. 2, pp. 257-273.

Langlois, R., N. (2007) "The entrepreneurial theory of the firm and the theory of the entrepreneurial firm.", *Journal of Management Studies*, Vol. 44, No. 7, pp. 1107 – 1124.

Lasch, F. and Yami, S. (2008) "The nature and focus of entrepreneurship research in France over the last decade: A French touch?", *Entrepreneurship: Theory and Practice*, Vol. 32, No. 2, pp. 339-360.

Lingane, A., and Olsen, S. (2004) "Guidelines for social return on investment.", *California Management Review*, Vol. 46, No. 3, pp. 116-135.

Mair, J. and Marti (2006) "Social entrepreneurship research: A source of explanation, prediction and delight.", *Journal of World Business*, Vol. 41, pp.36 – 44.

Martin, R., L. and Osberg, S. (2007) "Social Entrepreneurship: The case for definition.", *Stanford Social Innovation Review*, pp. 27 – 39.

Mort, G., J., Weerawardena, J. and Carnegie, K. (2003) "Social entrepreneurship: Towards conceptualization.", *International Journal of Nonprofit and Voluntary Sector Marketing*, Vol. 8, No. 1, pp. 76-88.

Nicholls, A. (2006) "Playing the field: A new approach to the meaning of social entrepreneurship.", *Social Enterprise Journal*, Vol. 2, pp.1-5.

Palmerino (1999) "Take qualitative approach to qualitative research.", *Marketing News*, Vol. 33, No. 12, pp. 35 – 36.

Peredo, A., M. and McLean, M. (2006) "Social entrepreneurship: A critical review of the concept.", *Journal of World Business*, Vol. 41, pp. 56-65.

Pomerantz, M (2003) "The business of social entrepreneurship in a "down economy".", *In Business*, Vol. 25, No. 3, pp. 25-30.

Prabhu, G., N. (1999) "Social entrepreneurial leadership.", Career *Development International*, Vol. 4, No. 3, pp.140-145.

Ridley-Duff, R. (2007) "Communitarian perspectives on social enterprise.", *Corporate Governance*, Vol. 15, No. 2, pp. 382-392.

Roper, J. and Cheney, G (2005) "Leadership, learning and human resource management: The meaning of social entrepreneurship today.", *Corporate Governance*, Vol. 5, No. 3, pp. 95-104.

Roberts, D. and Woods, C. (2005) "Changing the world on a shoestring: The concept of social entrepreneurship.", *University of Auckland Business Review*, Vol. 7, No. 1, pp. 45-51.

Roy, S. and Ghosh, L. (2008) ""Business as usual": A case study on the Body Shop.", *Journal of Applied Case Research*, Vol. 7, No. 2, pp.31-52.

Saunders, M., Lewis, P. and Thornhill, A.. (2007) *Research methods for business students*. London Prentice Hall.

Schicks, J. (2007) "Developmental impact and coexistence of sustainable and charitable microfinance institutions: Analyzing BancoSol and Grameen Bank.", *European Journal of Development Research*, Vol. 19, No. 4, pp.551-568.

Sillanpa, M. (1998) "The Body Shop values report – Toward integrated stakeholder auditing.", *Journal of Business Ethics*, Vol. 17, No. 13, pp. 1443-1456.

Social Enterprise Coalition. *Fifteen Restaurant*. [online]. Available from: http://www.socialenterprise.org.uk/pages/fifteen.html [accessed on 27/07/2010].

Tang, J. (2009) "Exploring the constitution of entrepreneurial alertness: The regulatory focus view.", *Journal of Small Business and Entrepreneurship*. Vol. 22, No. 3, pp. 221 – 238.

The Body Shop. *Values and campaigns*. [online]. Available from:http://www.thebodyshop.com/_en/_ww/values-campaigns/index.aspx [accessed on 27/07/2010].

Tracey, P., Phillips, N. and Haugh, H. (2005) "Beyond philanthropy: Community enterprise as a basis for corporate citizenship." *Journal of Business Ethics*, Vol. 58, No. 4, pp. 327-344.

Vidal, I (2005) "Social enterprise and social inclusion: Social enterprises in the sphere of work integration.", *Intl Journal of Public Administration*, Vol. 28, pp. 807-825.

Weerawardena, J. and Mort, G., S. (2006) "Investigating social entrepreneurship: A multidimensional model.", *Journal of World Business*, Vol. 41, pp. 21-35.

Wennekers, S. and Thurik, R., A. (1999) "Linking entrepreneurship and economic growth." *Small Business Economics*, Vol. 13, pp. 27-55.

Yunus, M. (2007) "Credit for the poor: Poverty as distant history.", *Harvard International Review*, Vol. 29, No.3, pp. 20-24.

Zahra, S.A., Gedajlovic, E., Neubaum, D.O. and Shulman, J.M. (2009), "A typology of social

entrepreneurs: Motives, search processes and ethical challenges.", *Journal of Business Venturing*, Vol. 24, No. 5, pp. 519-532.

Strategy for Social Enterprises or Never Say Never

Christos Apostolakis
Bournemouth Business School, Bournemouth University, UK

Abstract: The principal aim of this paper is to identify the strategic dimensions of an operational structure that could suit a social enterprise. Social entrepreneurship involves individuals and groups that create independent organisations in mobilising ideas and resources to address social needs. A focus on strategy in this context becomes paramount, as it can give a long-term direction to social enterprises and resolve some of its long-standing issues such as the position of social enterprises in being largely regarded as only suppliers to the state, often providing services for people. In this respect, a strategic framework is produced regarding aspects of mission, decision making power, profit distribution, effectiveness of service delivery and benefits for the local community. Methodology-wise the paper is based upon work that can be identified within the geographical context of Bournemouth, Poole and Christchurch, in Dorset, South West of England. It is based upon conduct of qualitative research including semi-structured interviewing, collection of secondary data and observations of local social enterprises. It is anticipated that potential research outcomes would include specific strategic practices in the way social enterprises operate and deliver services. It could also be suggested that strategies for the future should pay more attention into mobilising social enterprises as a force for innovation.

Keywords: strategy; social entrepreneurship; Bournemouth, Poole & Christchurch, UK; organisational operation;

1. Introduction

Through recent years social entrepreneurship has been hailed as contributing to unmet needs the state welfare system cannot normally meet. In this light, people who realise that there are opportunities to satisfy those needs gather the necessary resources and use them to make a difference (Thompson *et al*, 2000). In a world of injustice (Dorling, 2010)

Atherton (2004, in Anderson and Smith, 2007: 484) claims that "considerations of entrepreneurship are very much value driven". To this, Anderson and Smith (2007) add that socially accepted entrepreneurship practice can count as "authentic". In this respect, the political shift to engage the third sector in policy issues such as combating social exclusion since the late 1990s has meant that there is scope for involvement for this sector on entrepreneurial activities with a focus on supporting social interests (Aiken, 2006). Social enterprises could then be thought as particular types of organisation or activity that aim to mobilise resources from the community and from public/philanthropic sources but add an emphasis on securing resources in the form of trading income and an asset base (RISE, 2005).

As a concept social entrepreneurship is not new although it has begun to enjoy a higher media profile. According to Aiken (2006) this is because in a context of increased marketisation of social services there have been isomorphic pressures on social enterprises. Especially in Europe, the concept first appeared in the early 1990s with regard to the community and voluntary sectors, following a stimulus that began in Italy and was linked to the cooperative movement. Since then social entrepreneurship has gone through substantial development as a concept that has provided some very interesting examples of operational capacity. The author has been investigating social enterprises during the last four years and it is just lately he has been intrigued by the strategic scope the operation of a social enterprise might provide. This is what this paper attempts to exemplify: to suggest a particular strategic framework for social enterprises and test it via empirical research. As social entrepreneurship has been regarded still as a relatively novel subject area this makes the attempt even more intriguing: the unknown can always be attractive.

1.1.   When social entrepreneurship meets strategy

Defining social entrepreneurship activities could be almost exclusively based upon the context it is used for. Social Enterprise Coalition (2003: 7) identifies the concept as a

...business with primarily social objectives whose surpluses are principally reinvested for that purpose in the business or in the community, rather than being driven by the need to maximise profit for shareholders and owners.

In the UK social enterprises compete in the market place like any other business, no matter their business skills and knowledge to pursue social issues and achieve social goals. As Aiken (2006) suggests the operation of social enterprises indicates a focus on gaining resources in the kind of a public sector organisation that functions within a quasi market environment. On the other hand, an enterprise may undertake purely commercial trading activities such as building works or landscape gardening. Leadbeater (1997; cited by Thompson *et al*, 2000) suggests that the UK (and perhaps that of other countries too) welfare system is in need of radical reforms if it is to deal effectively with people's well-being and a significant contribution to this could be made via social innovations, that is new and creative community initiatives.

In addition, Defourny (2001; cited by Defourny and Nyssens, 2006: 6) suggest that the social dimensions of entrepreneurship can perhaps be encapsulated as follows:

- *An explicit aim to benefit the community:* One of the principal aims of social enterprises is to serve the community or a specific group of people. In the same perspective, a feature of social enterprises is their desire to promote a sense of social responsibility at local level;

- *An initiative launched by a group of citizens:* Social enterprises are the result of collective dynamics involving people belonging to a community or a group that shares a well defined need or aim;

- *A participatory nature, which involves the various parties affected by the activity:* Representation and participation of users or customers, stakeholder influence on decision-making and participative management are often important characteristics of social enterprises;

However, the exercise of measuring social entrepreneurship is a difficult task that cannot be resolved easily. This is due to the existence of a wide range of definitions about the object of investigation. Subsequently, not all social entrepreneurs will be working for revenues (either from grants or sales) and not all of these types of enterprises will become social. To this, someone would add that much of the discussion about social entrepreneurship has at its core a frustration about its effectiveness. Awareness of this frustration, as a principle driver of change can be very limited (Harding and Cowing, 2004).

One of the most important questions one needs to ask about social entrepreneurship is its capacity to create activities that could produce value for the people who can be benefited from this activity. Thus the next question is about how this value can be produced. According to Moon and Peery, Jr. (1997) this is the point in which entrepreneurship needs to be seen in conjunction with the subject of strategic management. This is because (social) entrepreneurship as a new field needs to borrow some analytical frameworks from other disciplines. Essentially, this is the point in which social entrepreneurship meets strategy. In addition, one would argue that the two subject areas are both dynamic entities concerned with organisational performance (Kuratko and Audretsch, 2009). Wickham (2006) points out that a strategy for entrepreneurial activities should:

- Encourage entrepreneurs to assess and articulate their own vision;
- Ensure auditing both of the enterprise and its environment;
- Illuminate new possibilities and freedom to explore them;
- Provide organisational focus;
- Guide the structuring of the organisation;
- Act as a guide to decision making;
- Provide a starting point for the setting of objectives;
- Act as a common language for the various stakeholders (ibid: 359-360).

In this light, vision, mission and strategy can perhaps become the ingredients of the same process, the world a (social) entrepreneur envisages in creating and developing (see Figure 1).

This process makes the entrepreneurial plans being put under the scope of management and thus creating the potential for becoming actual parts of an action plan. Moreover, in terms of the management process that could guide this strategy, Miles et al (2005) pinpoint that for an enterprise to become sufficient in its operation it is necessary to form a network atmosphere which could/should be shaped by: the use of operating protocols instead of hierarchical measures; a philosophy of minimal organisation; and the self-management of teams and firms – see Table 1 about effectiveness of service delivery.

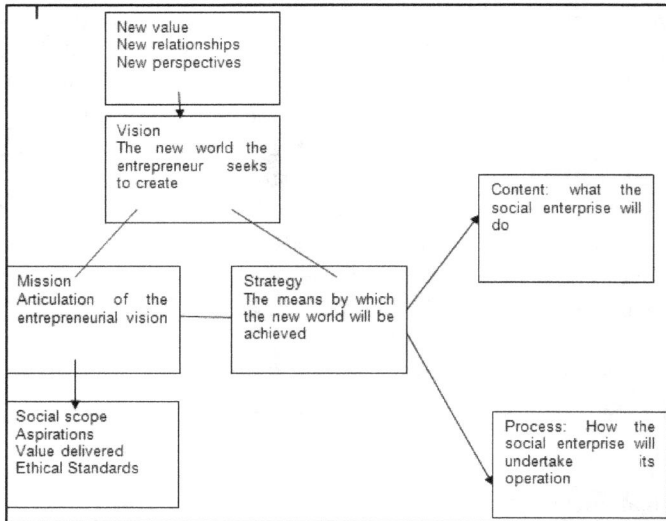

Figure 1: Vision, mission and strategy in the (social) entrepreneurial process Source: Adapted from Wickham, 2006: 361.

It could be argued that strategy is paramount for social enterprises as it is for every other type of organisation. As Johnson *et al* (2010) assert three key strategic choices for social entrepreneurs exist that shape their actions: *Social mission; organisational form* and *business model*. It is profound that similarities occur compared to the framework of Figure 1. These similarities begin with respect to the issue of having a well-established mission and go as far as getting a business model that in the case of this paper could be found in Table 1. After all, it is the implementation of a strategy that produces the actual results and needs to be well formulated. The point to be raised in here has to do with the actual operation of a social enterprise that could be identified within a strategy mindset. In this respect, it is worthwhile to examine which are the aspects that this process could take into consideration. As identified through the strategic framework of Figure 1 the mission of a social enterprise is a significant element that needs to be clearly defined. Stuart and Sorenson (2007) suggest that social status, opportunity identification and resource mobilisation are – cynically but realistically enough – the aspects that could define the attitude behind participation to an entrepreneurial activity. However, according to Ketchen et al (2007: 374) "discovering gold is only half of a firm's challenge – the firm must also find an effective way to mine the gold". Therefore, there is a certain need for balancing opportunity seeking with the way this opportunity could create an advantage for the enterprise. In this case, the advantage is an integral part of the social enterprise's mission. If the mission is defined then the balance of power and establishment of a sustainable equally nominated decision making process is necessary in order to support the core attribute or a set of attributes that can guarantee sustainable operation. Kuratko and Audretsch (2009) argue that in certain cases it is an organisational rejuvenation that is required in creating a superior organisational vehicle through which a strategy framework can be applied. Based on this strategy and organisational capacity it could be argued that if not profit distribution at least effectiveness in service delivery that could see some benefits for the local community could be founded.

With all the aforementioned in mind, the framework of operation is suggested in Table 1 and attempts to encapsulate and explain social enterprise activities in Dorset South West of England, primarily in the Bournemouth, Poole and Christchurch geographical area. This is not to suggest that this model cannot have universal applicability. It is just the acceptance that this is its initial and somehow experimental implementation in the context of social enterprises and it should be subject to testing its components in real-life conditions. A brief account of how social enterprises have been developed in the Bournemouth, Poole and Christchurch area is described in the next section.

Table 1: A strategy framework for social enterprises

Organisational Operation	
Mission of social entrepreneurs	A continuous activity of production of goods that incorporates a substantial degree of autonomy and collective mindset amongst participants
Decision making power	Representation and participation by all stakeholders including the end-user or customer and, participative management
Profit distribution	Although there is a certain degree of economic risk in establishing a social enterprise profit is distributed to a limited

Organisational Operation	
	extent, thus avoiding profit-maximising behaviour
Effectiveness of service delivery	Encapsulation of the desire to deliver a robust business performance shaped by social goals; ability for self-management within separate small-scale social enterprises
Benefits for the local community	The principal aim of a social enterprise that is shaped by the desire to promote a sense of social responsibility at local level

Source: *Adapting material from Defourny and Nyssens, (2006: 5 &6)*

2. Methodology

Methodology-wise the paper relies upon work that can be identified within the geographical context of Dorset and in particular of the conurbation of Bournemouth, Poole and Christchurch. In this respect, it was formatted around identification of the principal strategy models and frameworks that apply to social enterprise operation. It was decided to be qualitative. According to Mason (2002) qualitative type of research is grounded in its interpretivist nature to be concerned about the how a particular part of the social world is interpreted, understood and experienced. This was the reasoning for utilising the approach for the case of social enterprises in Bournemouth, Poole and Christchurch. At this initial stage of the research it was paramount to interpret and understand what social enterprises are and how they operate.

The research methods that were encountered were threefold: semi-structured interviews, secondary data and personal observations. This triangulation approach could make justice to the point of view made by Marshall and Rossman (1999) that such an approach can enhance generalisation of data. In this respect, ten semi-structured interviews were conducted that used respondents from various strands and organisations in order to establish a wide range of viewpoints at this very early stage. It has been envisaged that the next group of interviewees will include specifically managerial staff and volunteers from social enterprises in the Bournemouth, Poole and Christchurch area. Secondary data included reports and other archives about social entrepreneurship in the area material that was offered courtesy to Boscombe Link, one of the hubs for voluntary activity in the area. Personal observations included personal observations at the Boscombe Nursery, a branch of Sequal Solutions, one of the most developed social enterprises in the Bournemouth area. Nevertheless, this research method was used in supplementary capacity only.

In terms of limitations, it could be said that the researcher experienced some sort of "gate-keeping" issues. These could be perhaps explained as some form of "fear of the unknown" by the people of certain social enterprises, who never responded to requests for an interview by the researcher. They perhaps perceived his role as potentially interrogative. Having said this, this behaviour has to be tested again in the next phase of the research in which persistence on the researcher's part might be perhaps stronger.

3. Development of Social Entrepreneurship in Dorset

There are an increasing number of social enterprises in Dorset and the South West of England. As this paper refers to the initial part of research on strategy and social entrepreneurship it concentrates on the operation of social enterprises in the Bournemouth, Poole and Christchurch geographical area with the scope of expansion in the jurisdiction of Dorset and the South West of England later on. According to Regional Infrastructure for Social Enterprise (RISE) (2005) twelve sectors have been identified within which there are some successful examples of social enterprise in the Bournemouth, Poole and Christchurch area. Those cases have been identified under two types: a) the ones that are established to meet needs in the community, and therefore to provide goods and services such as childcare and social care, training and work experience or social housing; b) the ones that have been established to provide more democratic mobilisation by the community, to deal with issues of imbalance in the market for land and property or to engage in generating local investment to support enterprise in the community. Examples of this category include development trusts, community land trusts and community development finance initiatives. In this respect, existence of social enterprises fulfils governmental demands about offering better value for money compared with other service providers in certain fields such as social and child care, health and leisure (ibid.).

This paper investigates a range of social enterprises in the Bournemouth, Poole and Christchurch area such as Sequal Solutions and Dorset Reclaim. The former is a social enterprise which offers specialist support and services to businesses, individuals and communities – as they claim "to people who understand the real value of skilled help". Formed in May 2006 and trading as an official company since June 2006, Sequal is a wholly owned subsidiary of the Bournemouth Churches Housing Association group (Sequal Solutions, 2008). The company's mission is "to provide high quality services for the benefit of the community whilst finding new and innovative means of generating income" (ibid.). In addition, Dorset Reclaim began its operation in 1998 with the aim to: supplying low income families with good quality furniture, electrical and household goods; providing training and volunteering opportunities to help develop work and social skills; and encouraging local people to re-use and recycle, thereby reducing the amount going to landfill. At an indicative level they have so far: assisted over 18,000 families and individuals furnishing their homes; distributed over 100,600 items of furniture, electrical and household items; collected from more than 43,000 local people; and prevented more than 17,500 tonnes of household waste going to landfill. They are a registered charity and as such they operate in the social welfare market of Dorset as a voluntary organisation (Dorset Reclaim, 2010).

4. Discussion

The aim of this investigation is to analyse and interpret the research findings in a manner that can establish existence of a strategic framework for social enterprise activity in the Bournemouth, Poole and Christchurch area, in Dorset, South West of England. The principal questions to be answered are related to the framework of organisational operation as it has been identified above and how this applies to the context of the area under consideration. Specific organisational aspects that allow (or not) for effective service delivery will be looked at when the research reaches its later stages. This will enrich it further and contribute to a realistic account of strengths but also pitfalls that face the particular social enterprises. The paper identified the first initial findings in response to the particular framework under consideration.

With regard to the mission of social entrepreneurs in the Bournemouth, Poole and Christchurch area: According to RISE (2005) social enterprises normally have social and environmental aims such as job creation, training or the provision of local services. Their ethical issues may incorporate commitment to building skills in the community. In addition, the major principle is to reinvest their profit in order to achieve their social objectives. This statement seems to have affected the way social enterprises shape their aims in the area. For example, Sequal has identified their aims and mission as it follows:

"Our professional aims are clear. We're here to help re-invest the skills and experience of people used to dealing with life's challenges - and to open up opportunities they might otherwise miss. It is the mission of Sequal to provide high quality services for the benefit of the community whilst finding new and innovative means of generating income". (Sequal Solutions, 2008: electronic page on mission)

These aims have also been reflected in the way social enterprises seek appropriate staff/volunteers able to work as a team in acquiring experience and skills that then can be utilised for the benefit of the local community. It has to be admitted that it has not been evident how well this process works. Nevertheless, according to a health and disability advisor on employment for the local branch of the Department of Work and Pensions:

"We normally use the Council for Voluntary Services information to give people volunteer positions. Many social enterprises in the area advertise in that site for voluntary workers. So they tend to be highly represented in the organisations they are asking for voluntary workers. As for local businesses again we would be supporting clients on their path towards work in whatever form that would take in the most sustainable way possible. And obviously there are a few large-ish social enterprises in the area like Sequal that provides staff for many projects in the area such as the night shelter, couple of young people's bail hostels and drug and alcohol projects and kind of adult learning projects. I guess the perception would be because they are a social enterprise they will be more socially inclusive in their workforce maybe than a completely private organisation".

The fact that social enterprises like Dorset Reclaim offer opportunities for work experience through a structured volunteer programme is a good example of identifying and raising aspirations that align with the mission a social enterprise needs to acquire.

With respect to decision making power: It has come up according to the needs of the particular organisation. For instance, the author has observed the Sequal Childcare Neighbourhood Nursery at Boscombe and the way it has been run reflects a management-driven approach that assures effectiveness in dealing with children's day-to-day needs. According to the Ofsted (2011) inspection report for early years' provision it is necessary to have appropriate employment and vetting procedures in place that ensure all staff working with children are suitable to do so. Having said this, according to the report emphasis should be given on carrying out risk assessments when children are taken on outings.

Regarding profit distribution: The principle aim is to reinvest the profit in order to better provision of service for the community. It has to be said though that each social enterprise is obliged to look at how it manages the situation in an individual form of manner. For example, Dorset Reclaim has put an emphasis on increasing revenue through turnover, as opportunities for funding are not frequent. This is in line with the enterprise's ambition to remain self-financing, and not grant-dependent. Although suitable tendering opportunities are rather absent in the Dorset area potential public sector contracts e.g. for the collection and disposal of bulky household waste, have the potential to offer a valuable medium term source of income (Dorset Reclaim, 2009). According to SEDNET (2005) the annual turnover of voluntary organisations/social enterprises in the Boscombe & Springbourne area of Bournemouth was £12m in 2004/05.

Table 2: A strategy framework for social enterprises in the Bournemouth, Poole and Christchurch area

Organisational Operation of Social Enterprises in the Bournemouth & Poole Area		
	Ideally...	Bournemouth, Poole and Christchurch Area
Mission of social entrepreneurs	A continuous activity of production of goods that incorporates a substantial degree of autonomy and collective mindset amongst participants	Stated mission that claims provision of high quality services for the benefit of the community whilst finding innovative means of generating income
Decision making power	Representation and participation by all stakeholders including the end-user or customer and, participative management	It depends on the social enterprise and the provision of subsidies
Profit distribution	Although there is a certain degree of economic risk in establishing a social enterprise profit is distributed to a limited extent, thus avoiding profit-maximising behaviour	Again it depends on how marketised particular social enterprises are; more complex issues for voluntary sector based enterprises
Effectiveness of service delivery	Encapsulation of the desire to deliver a robust business performance shaped by social goals; ability for self-management within separate small-scale social enterprises	The delivery of services has been dependant on an accurate planning process plus efficient use of strategic planning tools, culture and attitude
Benefits for the local community	The principal aim of a social enterprise that is shaped by the desire to promote a sense of social responsibility at local level	The scope is there but the results are perhaps mixed

With regard to effectiveness of service delivery: The delivery of services has heavily relied upon accurate planning process plus efficient use of strategic planning tools such as balanced scorecard (RISE, 2005). There have also been issues with recruitment of volunteers as there seems to be a structural shift towards reliance on employed staff to deliver services. Service delivery has also been well affected by the culture and attitudes of each organisation (SEDNET, 2005). According to a university coordinator of business counselling in supporting enterprises in the area:

"As a background I think it all comes back to financial. We all advocate that the counselling should continue because that's how we can leverage the most, we can make an impact. I know in terms of our skills here we can bring overtime is very strong. And if we stop doing what we have been doing there are still going to be people coming in looking for the service and you know we are at the University and anything you do for students is a good thing. For the future, I really hope it will stay how it is because when you know that you are doing a good job in that stuff, you want to keep that going".

Regarding benefits for the local community: It seems that provision of benefits is dependent on the mission of the particular social enterprises and their way of looking for implementation of this mission. Volunteer aspirations and willingness to contribute to the local community are also major factors in achieving benefits for the common good. As a coordinator from Bournemouth University responsible for volunteering activities put it talking about a Community Champions' Programme event:

"There was a real rise of attitudes, you know for all of the community. It was quite impressive actually. It was really good to watch. And of course the champions are all geared up for being part of the community so it was a really, really powerful day. In terms of aspiration raising and being a student is not only about being a middle class intelligentsia. It has worked really well".

5. Conclusions

It seems that there are certain issues when it comes to the strategic development of social enterprises in the Bournemouth, Poole and Christchurch area. These issues range from inability to recruit volunteers, absence of young people from the ranks of volunteers up to ongoing funding issues (SEDNET, 2005). It seems that there are three key tasks to be undertaken for a strategy to become beneficial for social enterprises in the context of the Bournemouth, Poole and Christchurch area:

Christos Apostolakis

- A strategic planning process to be undertaken in order to reaffirm the core mission and aims of the strategic enterprise;

- Then to prepare a suitable business plan which would allow the organisation to fulfil their mission;

- Based on this to develop the organisational capacity in delivering the business plan;

- Finally, it is paramount to secure resources (both financial and human) in order to deliver the organisation's business plan (adapted from the Action plan; RISE 2005)

It could also be suggested that strategies for the future should pay more attention into mobilising social enterprises as a force for innovation. The key to this could be to commission for innovation more intelligently, either through strategic commissioning by local authorities, consumers or even more localised vehicles for investment in social innovation, such as environmental trusts. Denise Kingsmill (2010) questions the ability by (social) entrepreneurship to save the economy and become the answer to unemployment and asserts that perhaps the government is expecting too much from entrepreneurs. On the other side, it could be argued the social entrepreneurship should be never written off as it always finds a way to return with a different beneficial effect for the community. Never say never with social enterprises and how they have been developed in recent years.

References

Anderson, AR & Smith, R (2007) "The moral space in entrepreneurship: an exploration of ethical imperatives and the moral legitimacy of being enterprising" *Entrepreneurship & Regional Development* Vol. 19, November, 479-497

Aiken, M (2006) "Towards market or state? Tensions and opportunities in the evolutionary path of three UK social enterprises" in Nyssens, M. (ed.) *Social Enterprise – At the crossroads of market, public policies and civil society*, Routledge, London, pp. 259-271

Bournemouth University (2008) *Enterprise Review – Recommendations for improving the quality of Enterprise and Research support at Bournemouth University*

Defourny, J. & Nyssens, M. (2006) "Defining Social Enterprise" in Nyssens, M. (ed.) *Social Enterprise – At the crossroads of market, public policies and civil society*, Routledge, London, pp. 3-26

Dorling, D (2010) *Injustice; why social inequality persists*, The Policy Press, Bristol

Dorset Reclaim (2009) Business Plan 2009-2014 [accessed from the Internet on 19 June 2011] <URL: http://www.dorsetreclaim.org.uk/docs/businessplan.pdf >

Dorset Reclaim (2010) [No title] [accessed from the Internet on 15 April 2010] <URL: http://www.dorsetreclaim.org.uk/index.html>

Drayton, W. (2006) "Everyone a Changemaker – Social Entrepreneurship's Ultimate Goal" *Innovations*, Winter, pp. 80-96

Goss, D (2008) "Enterprise Ritual: A Theory of Entrepreneurial Emotion and Exchange" *British Journal of Management*, Vol. 19, No.2, pp. 120-137

Harding, R. & Cowing, M. (2004) *Social Entrepreneurship Monitor United Kingdom 2004*, London Business School, London

Johnson, G. Scholes K. & Whittington, R. (2010, 8th Ed) *Exploring Corporate Strategy*, Pearson Education Limited, Essex

Ketchen, DJ, Jr, Ireland, RD & Snow, CC (2007) "Strategic Entrepreneurship, Collaborative Innovation, and Wealth Creation" *Strategic Entrepreneurship Journal* Vol. 1, pp. 371-385

Kingsmill, D (2010) "On yer bike" all over again, *Management Today* 24th Sept 2010

Kuratko, DF & Audretsch, DB (2009) "Strategic Entrepreneurship: Exploring Different Perspectives of an Emerging Concept" *Entrepreneurship: Theory & Practice* January 2009, Vol. 33, Issue 1, pp. 1-17

Legge, J. & Hindle, K. (2004, 2nd Edition) *Entrepreneurship – Context, vision and planning*, Palgrave Macmillan, Basingstoke

Marshall, C & Rossman, G B (1999, 3rd edition) *Designing Qualitative Research* SAGE Publications, Thousand Oaks

Mason, J (2002, 2nd edition) *Qualitative Researching* SAGE Publications, London

McLeod, H. (1997) "The New Social Entrepreneurs" *Who Cares*, p.34

Miles R, Miles G & Charles C, (2005) *Collaborative Entrepreneurship: How Communities of Networked Firms Use Continuous Innovation to Create Economic Wealth* Stanford University Press: Palo Alto, CA

Moon, H C & Peery, NS Jr (1997) "Entrepreneurship in International Business: Concept, Strategy, and Implementation" *Entrepreneurship, Innovation, and Change* Vol. 6, No.1, pp. 5-20

Ofsted (2011) Sequal Childcare Neighbourhood Nursery at Boscombe (Inspection report for early years' provision)

Regional Infrastructure for Social Enterprise – RISE (2005) *Support for Social Enterprise in Bournemouth, Dorset and Poole* (Report compiled on behalf of the Dorset Community Action & Social Enterprise West)

Factors Influencing an Upscaling Process of Grassroots Innovations: Preliminary Evidence from India

Ann De Keersmaecker[1,2], **Prabhu Kandachar**[2], **Vikram Parmar**[2,3], **Koen Vandenbempt**[1] **and Chris Baelus**[1]

1 Design Sciences, Product Development, University of Antwerp, Antwerp, Belgium

2 Industrial Design Engineering, Delft University of Technology, Delft, The Netherlands

3 Venture Studio - Center for Innovative Business Design, Ahmedabad University, Ahmedabad, India

Abstract: People within low income markets have often shown their ability to identify their own problems and generate solutions. "Grassroots innovations" are ideas for products and services that respond to the constraint-based context and limited internal resources. Some of the grassroots innovators have converted their idea into a business. Upscaling a grassroots innovation has the potential to contribute to the regional socio-economic development and if nurtured properly, can be a significant force to empower local communities through inclusive development and job creation.

Although grassroots innovations have potential to become a commercial success, only in a limited number of cases the innovations have been implemented in the market. This paper focuses on the exploratory research carried out to identify and understand the factors that can influence the upscaling process of grassroots innovation. The research was conducted in two states in India, Gujarat and Rajasthan, by interviewing grassroots innovators and observing their innovations. Experiences of a selected list of organisations in India that are related to supporting grassroots innovators are taken into account in the research. These interviews revealed several opinions, needs, concerns and broader insights about the grassroots innovations. The findings were then transcribed, processed and structured. The analysis points out critical factors that influence the upscaling of grassroots innovations in India.

Earlier research had revealed that upscaling of grassroots innovations is often influenced by factors such as a lack of awareness on design and business approaches, poor entrepreneurial skills and a lack of start-up facilities in the given context. The current research contributes to this. We found that motivation of grassroots innovators, their perception and approach towards upscaling, overcoming isolation in local markets, possibilities to receive needed support and overcoming institutional formalisations are critical factors.

Keywords: grassroots innovation, entrepreneurship, upscaling, inclusive development, design efforts, emerging economies

1. Introduction

For more than 20 years, efforts are made to recognize grassroots innovations created in lower income markets (Gupta et al. 2003). Grassroots innovations are need-based products or services that are created by individuals or groups within local communities. They are often created in a resource constrained context typical of emerging economies and lower income markets (Kandachar and Halme 2008; Krämer and Belz 2008; Prahalad and Mashelkar 2010).

The innovations can address unsatisfied, sometimes collective needs (Butkeviciene 2009; Onwuegbuzie 2010) and challenges faced by citizens of such resource constrained regions. Thereby, grassroots innovators enable means of overcoming challenges that respond to local conditions (Onwuegbuzie 2010).

Grassroots innovations are similar to frugal innovations (Pansera 2012), which are popular in India and other countries in the global south, characterized by solutions that are low-cost, robust, easy to use and efficient. In contrast with frugal innovations targeting at large populations, grassroots innovations target at the moment at the innovator himself and/or a small and local population surrounding them, but with potential for larger populations.

The general trend in literature is the claim that grassroots innovations can contribute to a shift towards socially sustainable systems of consumption and production (Monaghan 2009), to a sustainable development in a country (Dutz 2007; Onwuegbuzie 2010) and to social change

(Butkeviciene 2009). Grassroots innovations can support the development of the people in the developing countries, providing a source of growth which hold potential for delivering economic development and inclusive innovation by improving local productivity, create more employment and income-earning opportunities (Dutz 2007), fostering social inclusion and empowerment and finally satisfy human needs (Butkeviciene 2009; Church 2005; Dutz 2007; Monaghan 2009; Onwuegbuzie 2010; Subba Rao 2006; Vinanchiarachi 2006). Furthermore, social impacts on a larger scale can be identified, such as entrepreneurial awareness-raising, education and promotion, changing the attitudes of local policy-makers, activating and engaging people and communities, and developing new ways of working towards social sustainable development (Church 2002, 2005). Although the potential for inclusive development is described, it remains unclear how these grassroots innovations can be upscaled effectively. Without upscaling effectively, the potential broader benefits of the grassroots innovation can be lost.

In practice, several attempts are carried out to upscale grassroots innovations. Although some examples of upscaled grassroots innovations are described, there is no formal investigation and documentation reporting the process of their upscaling (De Keersmaecker, Parmar, Kandachar, Baelus and Vandenbempt 2012). This explorative research focuses on identifying factors that influence this upscaling. Thereby, the research contributes to the understanding of the capabilities of the grassroots innovator himself/herself, and barriers and enablers for upscaling grassroots innovations.

2. Research questions and methodology

In order to understand how grassroots innovations can be upscaled, this explorative research seeks to identify factors influencing the upscaling of grassroots innovations in rural areas in India. The conducted research existed of two stages. First, preliminary desk research was carried out to create an initial overview of influencing factors. The desk research revealed three categories of factors that can influence upscaling of an innovation: context related factors, innovator related factors and innovation related factors (**Table 1**). This categorisation is based on a conceptual framework, integrating the array of variables defined in diffusion research to clarify their influence on an actor's decision to adopt an innovation (Wejnert 2002).

Table 1 Categorization of factors influencing upscaling of grassroots innovations before data collection

Context related factors	
Isolation: awareness and reachability	Connectedness with buyers, producers, distributors, financial and business development services and policy processes
Possibility to receive resources	Available resources: knowledge on engineering, business, design and financial, infrastructural and social resources (employees)
Freedom to operate	Formality of the business (influencing the possibility to finance the business) and intellectual property rights
Innovator related factors	
Motivation	Improving livelihood, economical drivers, escaping from poverty, social responsibility, ...
Entrepreneurial skills	Entrepreneurs are mean-driven (as opposed to goal-driven) and focus on achieving control without relying on predictions
Social status	Caste system, being respected by others in the neighbourhood
Innovation related factors	
Technical design decisions	Use of materials, production method, performance optimization, ...
Business plan related decisions	Target market, distribution method, financial plan, marketing, positioning towards competitors, ...
User related decisions	Including the latent and active needs

The overview of influencing factors functions as a basis to outline a semi-structured questionnaire to prepare for the second research stage: the field research. The questionnaire was prepared in such a way that also factors not defined by the desk research could be revealed. Therefore open-ended questions included questions pointing at the motivation and goals for innovating and doing the business, pointing at the grassroots innovators' role in upscaling and the opinion about the current upscaling process. By using contact summary sheets, main concepts, themes, issues and questions can guide the researcher during the interview (Miles and Huberman 1994).

The interviews were conducted in the states Gujarat and Rajasthan in India interviewing grassroots innovators (n=5). The grassroots innovators were visited at their small factory or workshop. Interviews were conducted by one researcher, in collaboration with a translator speaking the local language (Hindi and Gujarati), translating between the researcher and the grassroots innovator. Interviews were conducted following standardized qualitative research protocol (George and Bennett 2005; Yin 2003). Besides the questionnaire focussing on the influencing factors for upscaling, the grassroots innovation and the innovators' work environment were studied and observed to have supplementary, intangible information.

Furthermore, organisations in India that are related to supporting grassroots innovators are taken into account. Interviews with these organisations took place in their work environment.

All these interviews revealed several opinions, needs, concerns and broader insights of the context. The interviews were transcribed, analysed and content-coded. The data was analysed based on the transcriptions, the diary of the researcher containing reflections written down during field research and photographs made during the visits of the grassroots innovator and the organisations related to supporting. All these data were brought together and categorized. Later on, the factors detected during the analysis were compared with the factors defined during desk research. Reflection on this comparison led to the preliminary identification, specification and refinement of factors that influence the upscaling of grassroots innovations in India.

Research and preliminary findings presented in this paper are nevertheless subject to limitations. First, conducting interviews with a language translator, some information may have been lost or is misinterpreted by the translator, the interviewee or the interviewer. This issue has been triggered by discussing and reflecting with the translator on insights and thoughts immediately after every interview. Second, discussing the activities of the grassroots innovator or the supporting organisation can be tensed. The interviewees had often an understandable temptation to paint an exaggerated picture, or could only recollect vague memories. Verifying every statement on its correctness was not possible, but the triangulation method of comparing statements during the interviews and between different data collections helped interpreting them. Third, some grassroots innovators could have reacted with hesitation because they were confronted with an interviewer coming from another culture and with a different gender. The researcher tried to create trust and a relaxed atmosphere. Last, the research is based on a limited number of cases.

Although this is a condition to provide the depth required to generate rich descriptions of factors influencing upscaling, generalizability of case findings is limited. The purpose, however, is to illuminate opportunities and threats for upscaling grassroots innovations, in order to generate an in-depth and rich understanding of factors that influence this process.

3. Cases

The cases researched are a combination of grassroots innovators and their innovation (
and **Figure 1**), and organisations related to upscaling of grassroots innovations in India (**Table 3**).

Table 2 Description of grassroots innovations (the names used are pseudonyms)

Grassroots innovation	Bio-mass gasification	Cooling unit	Ploughing the field	Stripping cotton	Threshing crops
Industry	Energy	Household appliances	Agriculture	Agriculture	Agriculture
Novelty of the innovation	New technology, existing market	Existing technology, new market	New technology, new market	New technology, existing market	New technology, existing market
Development phase	Start-up firm, market phase, product improvements	Established firm, creating new product lines	Selling products, no official established firm, product optimization	Established firm, seeking for growth	Selling products, established firm, product optimization
Business marketing	B2B	B2C	B2B	B2B	B2B
Sales number last year	15 products	175 products	15 products	17 products	25 products
Informant	Relative of the innovator	Innovator & product manager (trainee)	Innovator	Innovator	Innovator

Selecting the grassroots innovations was done based on purposeful sampling. In dialogue with an organisation specialised in supporting grassroots innovations, grassroots innovations were selected based on experiences with upscaling.

Figure 1 Pictures of grassroots innovations (from left to right & from up to down showed in similar order as Table 2)

The organisations related to supporting grassroots innovators are either supporting effectively, supporting commissioned by another organisation, or seeking on how to support grassroots innovators.

The research is focussing on India because there is a considerable segment in the Indian market where grassroots innovations can flourish. This market segment exists of low income communities in resource constraint environments which is hardly been addressed. This research can contribute to serving Indian low income markets in resource constraint environments. Furthermore, India is an ideal environment to study grassroots innovations, because the Government of India has declared in 2010 the 'Decade of Innovation', and has set up of a National Innovation Council (NInC, www.innovationcouncil.gov.in) wherein a track is focussing on grassroots innovations, considered to nurture innovation in India.

Table 3 Description of organisations related to supporting grassroots innovators (the names used are pseudonyms)

Supporting organisation	Organisation supporting in Technology transfer in Asia	Small Indian design company	Big international design company	Organisation supporting Indian grassroots innovations	Organisation supporting Indian start-up entrepreneurs
Type of organisation	Intergovernmental organisation	Private organisation	Private organisation	Related to Indian government	Related to an Indian university
Motivation for support	Searching on how to support	Social motives	Social motives	Social motives	Searching on how to support
Type of support	Surveying organisations supporting formal start-ups	Redesign of a grassroots innovation	Redesign of some grassroots innovations	Engineering, business, IP, …	Support start-ups

4. Findings and reflections

After the data analysis, factors influencing upscaling of the grassroots innovation are grouped (**Table 4**).

Table 4 Categorization of factors influencing upscaling of grassroots innovations after data collection

Context related factors	
Isolation: awareness and reachability	Connectedness with potential markets
Possibilities to receive support and resources	Strategies to receive support
Freedom to operate	Formality of the business (influencing the possibility to finance the business) and intellectual property rights
Social context	Joint families with own cultural behaviour
Innovator and Innovation related factors	
Entrepreneurial skills	Entrepreneurs are mean-driven (as opposed to goal-driven) and focus on achieving control without relying on predictions
Design skills	Technical, business and user related decisions
Motivation	Interest to grow the business, acquiescence when others are copying, external encouragement to upscale

Categories were restructured, where Innovator and Innovation related factors are brought together because they are interrelated. Furthermore, the factor Social status became Social context and all Innovation related factors are shifted to Design skills. New detected influencing factors and additional insights are shown in **Table 4** and are described hereunder.

4.1. Context related factors

4.1.1. *Isolation: awareness and reachability*

First, grassroots innovators are isolated from the market. The grassroots innovation is often only produced and sold in the local context because the innovator is not aware and/or cannot reach potential markets. Not every grassroots innovation is scalable to an outer and cross-sectorial context; it depends on the need in that market and the supply and service chain available to reach that market. In case the grassroots innovation is scalable in another market (even from local to regional or national), this can mean a potential for upscaling, and will need an extra effort in the upscaling process (**Figure 2**). In most interviews, upscaling was perceived locally by the grassroots innovator, and the market outside his immediate vicinity was not seen as a potential market. Even if the grassroots innovator is already aware of a potential new market out the local context, he is often not familiar with how to reach and approach the market.

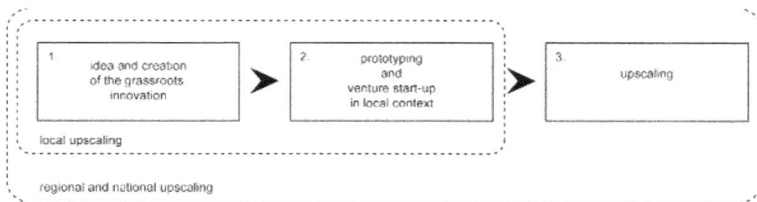

Figure 2: Upscaling process

Second, the grassroots innovator is in some cases not aware of the advantages and the possibilities to get support in upscaling his product, especially in the discipline of design.

Besides awareness of support and resources, reachability appears to be an issue. Except one organisation, most organisations related to supporting are targeting the middle and upper class, and expecting grassroots innovators to pay the fees, travel to and consult with the organisation, apply for the administrative procedures, etc. This is a barrier for the grassroots innovator to invoke support, although we found that his need and willingness to learn and/or collaborate to improve his business are clearly evident.

4.1.2. Possibilities to receive support and resources

Dependent of the capabilities of the grassroots innovator, and the typicalities of the grassroots innovation itself, case specific support is needed. There is not one generalizable need of the grassroots innovators; every innovator has his own problems and needs while upscaling his innovation. One grassroots innovator needs more support with understanding the market and user needs, the other with technological and production optimization or with improving the distribution channels, etc.

Support can be given in several ways to the grassroots innovator. During the field research, possibilities to build up and obtain knowledge are detected. The different scenarios of support offered are shown in Table 5.

Table 5 Scenarios for support

Scenario	In practice	Findings
Exchanging support between grassroots innovators	Exchange of experiences and best practices Some profit making grassroots innovators open their workshop for others	Accessibility to the workshops is complicated because grassroots innovators are living in isolated villages
Consulting a supporter	Supporters help with engineering and/or designing the innovation, or do market research Supporting organisations provide a compensation for the supporter, or support happens on a voluntary basis	The grassroots innovator should be involved actively, thinking and performing with the supporter, if not, support is not utilized effectively
Partnership with external business organisation	Collaboration by involving an established organisation during redesign, and seeking for collaboration in retailing	Venture capitalists and organisations showed their interest Partnering with business partners or retailers and negotiating proper agreements seems difficult

Studying these scenarios, it became clear that there needs to be a learning process for both the grassroots innovator and supporter or partner to learn from each other's expertise and context. The exchange of broader knowledge of the supporter, local knowledge of the grassroots innovator, and work executed together could give the ideal mixture of insights to upscale. **It is stated that grassroots innovators have** experiences, knowledge and deep understanding about what works in their local environments and what matters to local people (Agarwal 1983; Gupta et al. 2003; Onwuegbuzie 2010; Seyfang and Smith 2007).

Thus, a bilateral collaboration and learning process would be required to bring together technology, market and user insights to upscale the grassroots innovation.

During the research, it was observed that outsourcing a redesign activity, and then returning an optimized concept to the grassroots innovator was not effective. There needs to be a learning process for both grassroots innovator and supporter because they come from different backgrounds, not being aware of each other's context.

Formulating needs for support and making proper agreements between supporter or partner and grassroots innovator on the scenario for collaboration could help to make the support effectively deployed.

4.1.3. Freedom to operate

From the five organisations supporting grassroots innovations, one supports with filing for patenting. Anyhow, some grassroots innovations appeared to be copied. Furthermore, a grassroots innovator mentioned that his customer provides rental services with a purchased product during low seasons.

Although support in controlling and executing intellectual property rights (IPR) is offered, grassroots innovators resign themselves in the situation that is being copied.

Most grassroots innovators rather respond to this by innovating further, expanding their product and service portfolio. The grassroots innovator himself sometimes sees little value in these patents. Thus, these patents do not play a major role in creating barriers for the grassroots freedom to operate, what has an influence on the upscaling process.

Furthermore, formality of the business is an important aspect in terms of freedom to operate. Most grassroots innovators start selling their products without having a formal venture. Under a certain level of income, this is tolerated in India. When they grow further, most innovators are capable of forming their own venture, but struggle with administration and regulations to comply with the law. Depending on whether a firm is formal or informal, there are significant overall differences between how they finance their business, use bank accounts, and whether the entrepreneurs have loans for their businesses (Leino 2009).

Furthermore, some grassroots innovators are aware of quality controls and see value to apply for certificates because it can enhance selling numbers by convincing the customer of the quality. Applying for regulations like the ISO certificate (International Organization for Standardization) seems possible, but takes a lot of effort.

Patents, formalisation of the business and quality certificates can all influence the process of upscaling.

4.1.4. Social context

Grassroots innovators live in close communities and joint families and they have their own cultural and social values. Most observed grassroots innovators worked together with relatives and close neighbours. This can make it more difficult to be critical towards labourers and their quality of work, and makes the openness towards externals more difficult. By staying in close circles, it is more difficult to learn and exchange experiences. Collaboration with partners outside the local context takes time because of cultural differences, social status, language barriers, accessibility, etc.

In most cases, social values within the company were respected, creating a corresponding work environment. Nonetheless, in one case, aspects of child labour, defraud and deception were detected. These aspects have an influence on the social context and are most of the time not controlled and condemned by an executive power. In the end this leads to stagnating collaborations, influencing upscaling of the grassroots innovation.

4.2.   Innovator and innovation related factors

4.2.1. Entrepreneurial skills

Like every entrepreneur, grassroots innovators respond to an opportunity or challenge, inspired by the needs of people. During the research, it was recognized that some grassroots innovators were able to see a market opportunity, face time and financial limits for prototyping, diversify their product range, search for a unique selling proposition, and seek to create service and/or price competition.

These activities were not well-structured or organised, but this is linked to an entrepreneurial skill; being open for opportunities (Sarasvathy 2008).

Another recognized entrepreneurial skill is being aware of the risks, evaluating whether the downside of the risk is acceptable. Some grassroots innovators start selling their product when it is still in prototyping phase, anticipating on the reactions of customers, and later on acting accordingly.

Furthermore, grassroots innovators find solutions for various situations, remaining flexible and where needed leverage contingencies. For example, grassroots innovators arrange advance payments to purchase raw materials, organise distribution on the account of the customer and offer services like guarantees and after sales services, expecting that they will meet their promises, and otherwise anticipating on the situation.

In their local context, some grassroots innovators are capable of forming partnerships, and rely on human agency, which are all individual entrepreneurial skills (Sarasvathy 2008).

Some entrepreneurial skills are thus detected, but it is not possible to generalize this for all grassroots innovators, and to state that entrepreneurial skills are at its best. Upscaling is a process where entrepreneurial skills such as collaboration, partnerships, anticipating on unforeseen circumstances are needed.

4.2.2. Design skills

Referring to technological design decisions, the grassroots innovator obtains technological skills by self-education, observing other techniques and machines, and testing by trial and error. In some cases engineering support could optimize the product. The grassroots innovator uses local materials and in some cases finds the balance between second hand spare parts and new spare parts in order to meet the quality requirements. In one case, the grassroots innovator shifted to a larger city to have better resources nearby, like materials, and to strengthen their connectivity with customers and to expand commercial network.

Similarly to Jugaad innovation (Radjou, Prabhu, Ahuja and Roberts 2012), grassroots innovators use on-the-ground-feedback, rather than focus groups, to test the levels and acceptance of their innovation and make design decisions. They have a demand driven approach, responding to articulated needs of the market, and listen to customer feedback adapting their innovation accordingly. Furthermore, the grassroots innovator creates product alternatives depending on the customer's price/performance requirements, and sometimes make individual customized products. However, grassroots innovators are less aware of needs of *potential* users, especially outside their local context, which influences the possibilities for upscaling.

The business and marketing skills of the grassroots innovator are rudimentary. They rely on traditional methods like mouth to mouth communication and through advertising in the local newspaper, with minimal communication of the unique selling proposition. The customers addressed are mainly local. In our research, most of the grassroots innovators themselves articulated the need for marketing support.
Sometimes, the grassroots innovations are exhibited at a national fair, bringing all grassroots innovations together. Rather than facilitating real marketing activities, these fairs create acknowledgement of grassroots innovators' activities.

Furthermore, we found indications that business-to-business (B2B) marketing in low income markets understands the potential of grassroots innovations better than business-to-consumer (B2C) marketing. B2B could be a better marketing avenue than B2C. This needs however further research.

Design skills of the grassroots innovators are not at its best, and the innovator is often aware of this lack of skills. He indicated the need for support on business level, to quest potential new markets and corresponding distribution channels. The entire market itself, its market potential, and market entrance strategies are in most cases not known and the grassroots innovator is not familiar with corresponding activities. Upscaling the grassroots innovation needs optimized design skills.

4.2.3. Motivation

Motivation to create an innovation, start a venture around it and upscale, is of course needed. In the cases observed, different motivations were detected. Grassroots innovators were innovating and doing the business out of necessity, to earn their living, because they find joy in creating new things, because of social motives, to give something back to society, and to help their neighbours. In the case of social motives, the grassroots innovator seeks for upscaling in his local context because he is attached to that environment. The motivation to upscale in another context can be different.

The observed grassroots innovators show perseverance to persist with the business, also in difficult times. It is earlier identified that entrepreneurs who stay in business when forced to formalize and adapt to severe competition are the ones with motivation, innovations and entrepreneurial incentives (Stokanic 2009).

Furthermore, motivation to upscale is encouraged by attention from media and exposure through supporting organisations creating awareness and acknowledging and appreciating the grassroots innovators efforts.

In contrast, in some other cases, the grassroots innovator is more interested in innovating and designing the product than doing the business around it because they do not enjoy the process of upscaling for various reasons (too much effort, upscaling is not as fun as inventing etc.) (Nair 2012). In such cases, it is unclear how the grassroots innovation could get upscaled in potential markets.

5. Discussion

To comprehend the influencing factors for the upscaling of grassroots innovations, it is important to understand what people perceive as upscaling. During the interviews, there existed a distinction in upscaling depending on the interviewee: local upscaling, and regional or national upscaling (as shown in **Figure 2**). In the context of grassroots innovations, local upscaling refers to focusing energies and resources on achieving greater impact in the same location where the enterprise was started. Regional and national upscaling refers to the growth in business by expanding a grassroots innovation to other geographic locations. Local upscaling of grassroots innovations is to some extent happening at the moment. This interpretation of upscaling is related to the isolation and the lack of awareness from potential markets as described before.

Regarding the perception of upscaling, upscaling can be understood as doing the business, or let the grassroots innovation been copied. The research revealed in some cases acquiescence of the grassroots innovator when others are copying his grassroots innovation. Depending on the motivation, some grassroots innovators are fine with copying their idea, hoping that others can benefit from the product and its business too. This also imposes a new way of interpreting upscaling. Grassroots innovations copied by other entrepreneurs can improve organically, benefitting a larger population than when protected by IPR. Research is going on at the moment on how an innovation can be copied in an informal context, and can get optimised and embedded locally (Gómez-Galvarriato Freer 2012).

A concern while upscaling a grassroots innovation regionally or nationally is how to translate the innovation. In case of translating an innovation to another context, it needs to be assessed whether the local innovation could be replicated and/or should be customized (Soman, Kumar, Metcalfe and Wong 2012). In case of replicating, the grassroots innovation should be assessed on whether the innovation and its business are paramount and can be transcended in a new region and context, taking into account all factors that influence upscaling and that could be specific to the region where the grassroots innovation emerged, like production method, use of local materials, existing providers and competitors, etc. In case the grassroots innovation should be customized as per the new region, it is a matter of assessing whether the investment in customizing by redesigning to the new context, culture, norms and practices, is worth the effort. Therefore, it is important to evaluate the feasibility of upscaling in another region and context taking into account the components of the grassroots innovation that should be adapted or modified.

6. Conclusion

Earlier research had revealed that upscaling of grassroots innovations is often influenced by factors such as a lack of awareness on design and business approaches, poor entrepreneurial skills and a lack of start-up facilities in the given context (De Keersmaecker et al. 2012). The current research contributes to this. We found that motivation of grassroots innovators, their perception and approach towards upscaling, overcoming isolation in local markets, possibilities to receive needed support and overcoming institutional formalisations are also critical factors.

Furthermore, as assumed before, most grassroots innovations are addressing the lower income markets, although not directly. Grassroots innovations are addressing these markets indirectly by creating employment and functioning as an example for others to innovate.

With this preliminary evidence, it is recommended to focus further research on validating the research insights with more upscaled and not (yet) upscaled cases. An additional avenue for research is investigating which factors are determinative in influencing an upscaling process of grassroots innovations and the causal links between these factors in order to understand how the upscaling process can be influenced effectively.

For this research, a certificate of merit was awarded at the 8th European Conference on Innovation and Entrepreneurship September 19-20, 2013.

References

Agarwal, B. (1983) "Diffusion of Rural Innovations: Some Analytical Issues and the Case of Wood-burning stoves", *World Development*, 359-376.

Butkeviciene, E. (2009) "Social innovations in rural communities: methodological frameworkand empirical evidence", *Social Sciences, 63*, 80-88.

Church, C. (2002) *The Quiet Revolution*, Birmingham: Shell Better Britain.

Church, C. (2005) Sustainability: the importance of grassroots initiatives (Summary of Presentation ed.). London: Community Environment Associates.

De Keersmaecker, A., Parmar, V., Kandachar, P., Baelus, C. and Vandenbempt, K. (2012) Towards Scaling Up Grassroots Innovations in India: a Preliminary Framework, *International UNESCO Chair Conference*. Lausanne.

Dutz, M. A. (2007) *Unleashing India's Innovation*.

George, A. L. and Bennett, A. (2005) *Case Studies and Theory Development in the Social Sciences*, Massachusetts: MIT Press.

Gómez-Galvarriato Freer, M. (2012) From informal to water-sustainable, from water-sustainable to water-provider, *International PLEA Conference Opportunities, limits & needs - Towards an environmentally responsible architecture*. Lima, Peru.

Gupta, A., Sinha, R., Koradia, D., Patel, R., Parmar, M. and Rohit, P. (2003) "Mobilizing grassroots' technological innovations and traditional knowledge, values and institutions: articulating social and ethical capital", *Futures, 35*, 975-987.

Kandachar, P. and Halme, M. (2008) Farewell to pyramids: how can business and technology help to eradicate poverty? In P. Kandachar & M. Halme (Eds.), *Sustainability Challenges and Solutions at the Base of the Pyramid: Business, Technology and the Poor*, UK: Greenleaf Publishing.

Krämer, A. and Belz, F.-M. (2008) Consumer integration into innovation processes, a new approach for creating and enhancing innovations for the base of the pyramid. In P. Kandachar & M. Halme (Eds.), *Sustainability Challenges and Solutions at the Base of the Pyramid* (pp. 214-241), UK: Greenleaf Publishing.

Leino, J. (2009). *Formal and Informal Microenterprises*: The World Bank.

Miles, M. B. and Huberman, A. M. (1994) *Data Management and Analysis Methods*, London: Sage Publications.

Monaghan, A. (2009) "Conceptual niche management of grassroots innovation for sustainability: the case of body disposal practices in the UK", *Technological Forecasting & Social Change, 76*, 1026-1043.

Nair, A. K. (2012) Grassroots Innovations In A. De Keersmaecker (Ed.).

Onwuegbuzie, H. (2010) Sustainable Development Strategy Using Indigenous Knowledge and Entrepreneurship. Lagos: Lagos Business School & Pan-African University.

Pansera, M. (2012) "Eco-innovation as a Development Tool: Evidence from Latin America and Asia", Paper presented at the Third International Conference on Degrowth: Ecological Sustainability and Social Equity, Venice.

Prahalad, C. K. and Mashelkar, R. A. (2010) "Innovation's Holy Grail", *Harvard Business Review*, 2-10.

Radjou, N., Prabhu, J., Ahuja, S. and Roberts, K. (2012) *Jugaad Innovation: Think Frugal, Be Flexible, Generate Breakthrough Growth* San Francisco: Jossey-Bass.

Sarasvathy, S. D. (2008) *Effectuation: Elements of Entrepreneurial Expertise*, Cheltenham: Edward Elgar Publishing.

Seyfang, G. and Smith, A. (2007) "Grassroots innovations for sustainable development: towards a new research and policy agenda", *Environmental Politics*, 584-603.

Soman, D., Kumar, V., Metcalfe, M. and Wong, J. (2012). Beyond Great Ideas: A Framework for Scaling Local Innovations. *Rotman Magazine, Fall 2012,* 50-55.

Stokanic, D. (2009). *Entrepreneurship on the margin between informality and formality: The textile industry in South-West Serbia.* Budapest: Central European University, Department of Socialogy and Social Anthropology.

Subba Rao, S. (2006) "Indigenous knowledge organization: an Indian scenario", *International Journal of Information Management, 26,* 224-233.

Vinanchiarachi, J. (2006) Grassroots Innovations Serving as Rural Growth Impulses In n. f. edited (Ed.), *International Association of Management of Technology.* Beijing.

Wejnert, B. (2002) "Integrating Models of Diffusion of Innovations: A Conceptual Framework", *Annual Review of Sociology, 28,* 297-326.

Yin, R. (2003) *Case Study Research, Design and Methods* (Third ed.), United States of America: Sage Publications.

Social Technologies for Increasing Entrepreneurship in Public Administration Organizations

Aelita Skaržauskienė

Faculty of Social Informatics, Mykolas Romeris University, Vilnius, Lithuania

Abstract: Today`s organizations are increasingly finding themselves in a world characterized by globalization, turbulence and complexity, paralleled with an exponential advancement in information technology (IT). These conditions require flexibility, collaboration, innovation and the courage to embrace uncertainty and ambiguity. Such extreme challenges require radical solutions and the transformation of organization development. Improving efficiency and effectiveness in the knowledge-intensive society demands sophisticated technologies – learning from and solving problems with other people in organisations using new technologies. Social technologies (ST) are a powerful tool for holding organizations accountable for their social impact. Information technology has experienced many cycles of innovation, always producing more complex and integrated sets of technologies to respond directly to societal needs. The paper presents new management practices using social technologies in public administration organizations for addressing complexity, uncertainty and changes. Drawing on qualitative and quantitative evidence the paper is seeking to improve our understanding of the role of social technologies and to give guidance on how to handle the relationship between technologies and entrepreneurship in public administration organizations.

Keywords: social technologies, knowledge management, innovation, entrepreneurship

1. Introduction

Social technologies have the potential to provide individuals with significant economic and non-economic benefits. As people multiply their abilities to organize themselves through social technologies, there is a possibility to effect positive change in communities and governments, and to help communities collaborate in non-political ways, such as organising disaster aid. Social technologies, for example, were an important enabler of the 2011 Arab Spring (Bughin, et al., 2011, Divol et al, 2012). ST can be disruptive to existing power structures (corporate and governmental). Despite the rapid adoption of social technologies, far more growth lies ahead. Today, more than 80 percent of the world`s online population is interacting with social networks on a regular basis, but 65 percent of the world population – 4.6 billion people – still lack internet access (Chui et al., 2012). It is a fact that organizations have only started to appreciate the potential of social technologies in recent years. Tools like Facebook, Twitter, and LinkedIn appeared with personal use, but recent surveys have demonstrated that inside an organization, users employ social technologies to improve their job, and not just for personal matters (Forrester Research, 2009). Today organizations are very complex environments. Information technology has experienced many cycles of innovation, always producing more complex and integrated sets of technologies to respond directly to society needs (Koplowitz, 2010). In spite of this, the huge quantity of documents produced daily can create innumerable silos of information. As a consequence, knowledge capture and sharing can be too difficult and ineffective (Alberghini et al., 2010). New technologies could contribute to developing an environment conducive to building and nurturing relationships among organization members and increasing entrepreneurship. Further, managers could facilitate the creation of organizational capabilities using technologies such as the ability to locate and share knowledge rapidly and respond to changes. Knowledge held by employees and the network of relationships help dynamically to solve problems and create new knowledge.

The paper presents new management practices using ST in public administration organizations to address complexity, uncertainty and changes. Drawing on quantitative evidence the paper seeks to improve our understanding of the role of social technologies and give guidance on how to handle the relationship between technologies and entrepreneurship in public administration organizations.

2. Defining social technologies

The term "social technology" was first used by A. W. Small and Ch. R. Henderson at the University of Chicago around the end of the 19th century (Wikipedia, 2012). Small (1898) defined "social technology" as being the use of knowledge of the facts and laws of social life to bring about rational social aims. Henderson (1895) used the term "social art" for methods by which improvements to society are and may be introduced; social scientists are the ones who make predictions and social art is what gives directions. According to Li and Bernoff (2011) "social technology" is a term that has had two meanings historically: as a term related to "social engineering", it emerged in the 19th century (Schotter, 1981; Sugden, 1989; North and Wallis, 1994; Nelson, 2008; Pelikan, 2003, Leichteris, 2011) and as a description of "social software", it appeared in the early 21st century (Sproull and Faraj, 1997; Johannessen et al., 2001; Andersen, 2011; Duarte, 2011; Leibetseder, 2011; Chui et al, 2012; Derksen et al, 2012). McKinsey Global institute (2012) defines social technologies as digital technologies used by people to interact socially and together to create, enhance, and exchange content. Social technologies distinguish themselves through the following three characteristics (Chui et al., 2012):

- They are enabled by information technology;
- They provide distributed rights to create, add, and/or modify content and communications;
- They enable distributed access to consume content and communications.

In modern understanding of social technology, it was referred to any technology application for various purposes, especially to support a decision making process, so in the sense of *technology* "social technologies" are instantly recognized via some kind of media. Koo et al. (2011) present five media types of the new generation: "telephone is representing a traditional medium; video conferencing, email, and instant messenger representing computer-mediated technologies; and blog and social networks representing new social media". Communication technologies such as telephone, voice mail, e-mail, videoconferencing, and instant messaging help members of virtual teams or groups stay in touch with one another and share information. All these types of media or technologies can be described in terms of three dimensions (Johannessen et al., 2001):

- • *Richness:* the ability to convey verbal and nonverbal cues, and facilitate shared meaning in a timely manner;
- • *Interactivity:* the extent to which rapid feedback is allowed;
- •*Social presence:* the degree to which virtual team members feel close to one another.

Surveys conducted by analysts such as Forrester Research (2012) demonstrate that social technologies continue to grow in popularity inside the society; adoption of wiki in particular is in the leading position, followed by social networks. Nowadays, when people think about social technologies, they often refer to Web applications like Facebook or LinkedIn, even though family, friends, classmates, or network of work colleagues remain the most common social networks (SN). This misconception has even a scientific base. Social technologies include a wide range of applications that can be used by consumers, private or public sector organizations, or as an interaction tool between those subjects. They include many of the technologies that are classified as "social media", "Web 2.0", and "collaboration tools". Social gaming, social art, crowdsourcing, discussion forums could also be defined as social technologies. However, after the fundamental exploitation in this area, the current function of social technology is to serve social purposes.

Although the term "social communication technologies" is most commonly used to refer to new social media, a redefinition of this concept based on the original definition is needed. Nowadays the concept of "social technology" has several aspects which destabilize the dominant image of technology. It emphasizes the social sciences and humanities as society shapers, reconsiders the strength of "soft technologies" and restores focus on human actors in sociotechnological assemblages without making them their sovereign masters (Derksen, 2012). That means social technology is increasingly salient as an object of study for the social sciences: sociality is more and more something that people create technically. The instrumental, technoscientific approach to social life is not the exclusive province of social scientists anymore, but by the same token, it demands all the more attention as an object of study (Mayer, 2009). Social technologies are defined as any technologies used for social purposes or with a social basis, including social hardware (traditional communication media), social software (computer mediated media), and social media (social networking tools) (Helmer et al., 1966; Alberghini, et al., 2010).

3. Social technologies for increasing entrepreneurship

The growth of the Web in reach and capability and as a medium for interaction set the stage for the explosive growth of social technologies. Social technologies unleash creative forces among users and enable new relationships and group Dynamics (Chui et al., 2012). Social technologies are becoming the preferred method of communication of new generations and communication styles are evolving into a more collaborative approach (Alberghini, et al., 2010). In a more and more hyperactive world, people could feel immediate benefits in connecting with the right peers, getting answers to questions and finding information. "The real power of technologies stems from the innate appeal of interacting socially and the pleasure and intellectual stimulation that people derive from sharing what they know, expressing opinions, and learning what other know and think" (Chui et al, 2012). As has been seen in early use of social technologies, when these ways of interacting are applied to commercial and professional activities (e.g. developing and selling products, working together to solve a business problem), the resulting value creation is impressive (Bughin et al., 2011).

Modern organizations face new challenges: a growing swarm of unconventional rivals, crumbling entry barriers, a rapid transition from the "knowledge economy" to the "creative economy," intensifying competition for talent and a profusion of new stakeholder demands (Divol, et al., 2012). To tackle these challenges, organizations will need to become far more adaptable, innovative, inspiring and accountable than they are right now. This will require a fundamental re-tooling of traditional management practices. Management strategies need to shift from command and control to sense and respond (Rao, 2005). The Millennials, also known as the Millennial Generation (Generation Y), are people born between 1980 and 2000. They are now entering the workplace and have habits and communication forms different from the older generation workforce. According to Forrester analysts De Gennaro and Fenwick, there are key trends that will make the inclusion of social technology a necessity in the societal life. These trends are the physical distance between teams and the entrance of Millennials into the workforce (De Gennaro, 2010).

These new employees bring very different understanding of entrepreneurship, different needs, experiences and expectations to the job and often meet a seasoned workforce that has very different work styles (Schooley, 2009). Anyway, what Millennials want to support in their work – flexible work schedules, social media tools, or a collaborative environment – are the work features that other employees can benefit from, too (Schooley, 2008). New technologies allow people to ask questions, share ideas and discover people skills regardless of the hierarchy. These tools help to break down organizational and cultural barriers such as time differences (Koplowitz and Owens, 2010). Freed from the limitations of the physical world, people are able to use social technologies to connect across geographies and time zones and multiply their influence beyond the number of people they could otherwise reach. These new opportunities enable new forms of entrepreneurship. In social networks all members are able to contribute to content building, which is distributed freely and instantaneously, so from leader-centered approach in management we move to distributed leadership, from top-down management to bottom – up management. Social interaction is a powerful way to efficiently organize knowledge, culture, economics and political power. While the typical corporation is based on a center-to-end architecture, in which decision-making authority is heavily concentrated at the top, the Web is built on an end-to-end architecture, where power is highly distributed (Divol, 2012). Within the new competitive situation, a critical issue facing entrepreneurs, is how to manage an unpredictable and unstable future. Since the future is basically unpredictable and uncertain, evoking images, rather than established facts, organizations must rely on creative initiatives from the employees to be able to create the desired future (Johannessen, 2001). Software developers have continued to develop tools for creating new interaction possibilities (Jue et al., 2009). Gamefication, the use of features of games to enhance online engagement, is another way how social technologies can encourage increased collaboration. Therefore, increasing entrepreneurship in the knowledge-intensive society demand sophisticated technologies – learning from and solving problems, creating and building business ideas with other people (Cross et al., 2001).

Today`s public administration organizations change the focus from the ineffective bureaucratic models onto more flexible communities of professional workers such as online communities, virtual self-managing teams, networked organizations, etc. Social technologies enable social behaviours to take place online, endowing the interactions with the scale, speed, and disruptive economics of the Internet (Chui et al., 2012). Over the last decade, the Internet has had a profound impact on entrepreneurship. It has spawned a slew of new management models and has helped make operating models vastly more efficient. Social media/networking and the collection of tools they have spawned have moved solidly into the strategy toolbox for public administration organizations. Many strategies taken to increase entrepreneurship with social technologies by private-sector companies also apply to the public sector. However, the operating models and mission of public administration organizations are distinct from those of business enterprises. Therefore, we have identified some social technological concepts that are mandatory for every public administration organization today, see Table 1 (Zupan, Kase, 2007; Klososky, 2011; Chui et al., 2012; Divol, 2012):

Table 1: Social technologies increase entrepreneurship in public administration organizations

Collection of information and insights	Gather information
	Build Rivers of Information
	Crowdsource recourses and solutions
	Analyse data
Mobilizing structures	Fundraise
	Create and expand volunteer network
	Retain support
Mission execution	Educate the public
	Engage supporters
Organization management	Improve collaboration and communication
	Distribute leadership
	Participate in collective decision making process
	Create self-managing networked teams
	Rapid organizing
	Adapt gamefication
Learning and training	Increase e-learning
	Match talents to roles

Organizational Voice	Conversation with constituents, mindshare
Online Reputation Management (ORM)	Form online reputation, all comments become searchable
Marketing	Use crowdsourcing
	Increase creativity

4. Research results

The paper follows a quantitative research approach. The total sample consists of 122 respondents. The sample was at random selected in Lithuanian Public sector organizations such as Ministries and Departments. The two stage procedure, recommended by Bartlett, Kotrlik and Chadwick (2001) was employed to determine a sample size of every subsample. Firstly, sample size of 100 was determined using sample size table and having in mind that the population size is over 10000 and data is continuous. Secondly, having collected 100 responses, the worst variances were identified in every subsample. Finally, the size of every subsample was calculated using formula recommended by Bartlett, Kotrlik and Chadwick (2001). Mainly public heads of departments and managers were surveyed using a web-based questionnaire. Data was analyzed using statistical software package SPSS. The questionnaire ends with demographic questions. The return rate of the survey was 55% and can be treated as good.

It is interesting to note that all the participants answered positively (yes or no option) the question "Do you believe that technologies are applicable to all types of organizations, regardless of the field they operate?" 75% of the respondents reported using some form of social technology in their organization. Of these more than 60% indicated benefits from social technologies. The heaviest users of technologies are the users between the age 25 - 35.

Online reputation management is the most common organization application in public administration organization (see Figure 1), while marketing remains the most popular application in business according to Chui et al. (2012). More than half of the respondents admit that they use social technologies to strengthen their organizational voice (56%) and for collecting information and insights (69%).

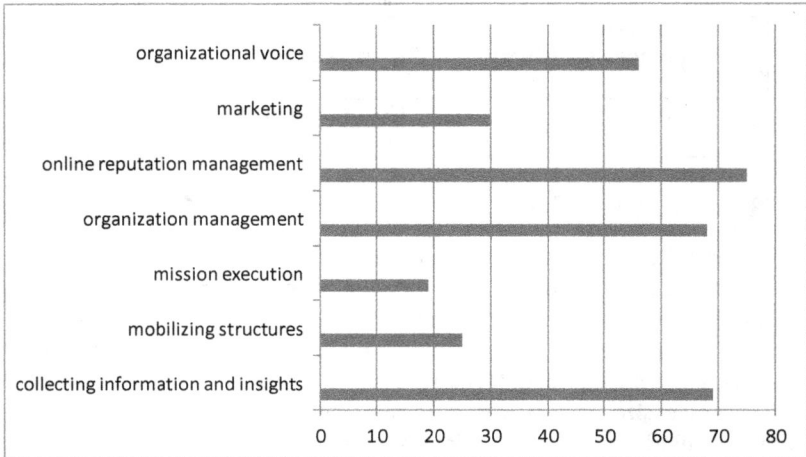

Figure 1: The use of social technologies across functions

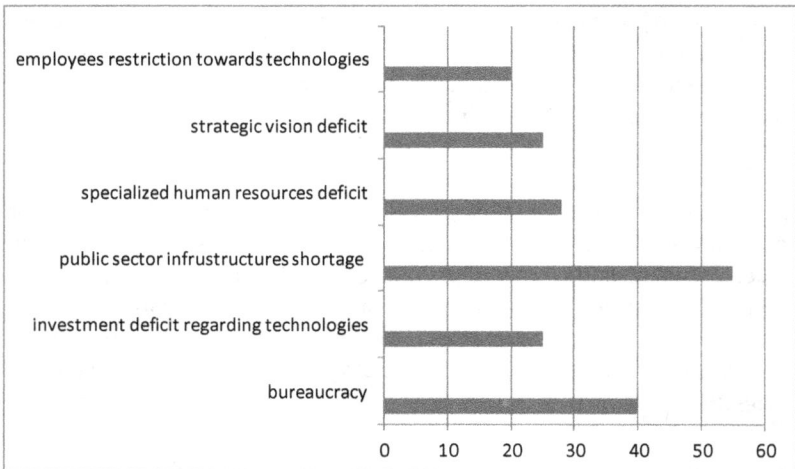

Figure 2: The most important obstacles preventing application of new technologies

The respondents reported benefits from the use of social technologies for various purposes: first of all, reducing communication costs (80%), increased speed to access knowledge (68%), decreasing travel costs (64%), increasing employees' satisfaction (34%). The analysis of the most important obstacles to organization in order to adapt to new technologies shows that the most commonly mentioned are bureaucracy, investment deficit, infrastructure shortage, etc. (see Figure 2.)

5. Limitations

The references used for this survey are not an exhaustive list within the topic area. Relevant sources of information may also exist in other domains of scientific inquiry. Because of the chosen research approach, the research results may lack generalizability. The sample of this research was limited only to national level; therefore there is no possibility to compare results across different countries.

6. Discussion and conclusions: The Potential and Risks of Social Technologies

Business enterprises that apply social tools have reported measurable business benefits (McCinsey, 2012). Our research results show growing interest of public administration organizations in social technologies and increase of entrepreneurship in these organizations by interaction of the staff and outside partners, citizens and society. Public administration organizations are usually companies with high numbers of employees and the incorporation of social tools can be used to facilitate collaboration and co-creation, reduce the time spent in unnecessary in-person meetings, and help share internal knowledge and best practices. Organizations can also use ST to hire new employees and integrate contractors or experts into networked teams. From almost any location employees could initiate projects, form teams and complete their tasks. The conducted research indicated that the main obstacles to apply technologies are bureaucracy, investment deficit, infrastructure shortage for public administration.

New technologies allow people to connect at a different scale and create a unified, powerful voice – as social groups or entire societies – that can have significant impact on the ways in which dialogues are shaped and policy is made (Chui et al., 2011). Social networking capabilities are providing vital information in a way that is adaptive and user-driven.

However, all these technologies have limitations that can easily lead to misinterpretation. They cannot provide the same richness as face-to-face interaction. Because of delays in transmission and the lack of social and nonverbal cues, communication technologies can interfere with open communication, knowledge sharing, and the ability of teams to identify and resolve misunderstandings. Online collaboration, in its current state, is not a very good substitute for face-to-face interactions that are critical to create innovations, improve organizational climate, foster human relationships, motivate and inspire. Furthermore, the older generation tends to be sceptical about social technologies, so it is important to implement something very useful for all society members and that should become a habit and a necessity at work and private life. For this reason, it is necessary to monitor the user engagement and to educate the community for using social technologies (Allberghini et al., 2010).

The use of social technologies can also carry risks. One risk is the possibility of abuse, such as excessive employee time spent "chatting" about non-work-related topics on internal or external social networks or using social media to attack fellow employees or management. Enterprises have taken different approaches to handling this risk, from forbidding non-work-related conversations or censoring critical opinions to welcoming the critiques and engaging in public conversation with the critics. Other risks involve breaches of customer privacy. Similarly, there is a great need for information security, but an organization's need to maintain data security can limit the ways in which social technologies can be applied. In addition, in many nations, censorship and restrictions on Internet use stand in the way of value creation by organizations that hope to enable citizens to interact with them and that wish to harvest deep insights from social data (Klososky, 2011; Chui et al., 2012; Divol, 2012).

With social technology, more and more users are becoming a part of the global conversation, creating their own content rather than just consuming it. However, the quality of user-generated content varies dramatically – from excellent works of journalism to spam and even abuse (Bauerlein, 2008). Some critics have argued that the short-form content available through social technologies is making people less able to digest large and complex amounts of information. The opposing view is that even our existing means of content selection do not always assure quality, that the diversity of opinions is healthy and increase creativity and critical thinking (Carr, 2010).

Our final discussion about the potential and risks of "social technologies" will be the occasion to address through theoretical and conceptual reflections and empirically-oriented contributions the following questions: How technologies are changing society`s life? Which social technologies are especially prominent in contemporary culture, and how can we study these?

References

Alberghini E., Cricelli L., Grimaldi M. (2010) "Implementing knowledge management through IT opportunities: definition of a theoretical model based on tools and processes classification", *The Proceedings of the 2nd European Conference on Intellectual Capital*, Lisbon, Portugal, 29-30 March, 2010, pp. 22-33.

Andersen, K. N. (2011) "Social Technologies and Health Care: Public Sector Receding, Patients at the Steering Wheel?", *Social Technologies '11: ICT for Social transformations'*, 17-18 November, 2011, Vilnius-Net.

Bauerlein, M. (2008) *The Dumbest Generation,* New York: Penguin Group.

Bartlett, J.E., Kotrlik, J.W., Higgins, Ch. C. (2001) "Organizational research: determining appropriate sample size in survey research", *Information Technology, Learning and Performance Journal,* Vol. 19, No. 1, pp. 43-50.

Bughin, J., Byers, A.H., Chui, M. (2011) "How social technologies are extending the organization", November, *McKinsey Global Institute.*

Carr, N. (2010) *The shallows: What the Internet is doing to our brains,* New York:

Chui, M. et al, (2012) "The Social Economy: Unlocking Value and Productivity Through Social Technologies", *McKinsey Global Institute Report.*

Cross, R., et al. (2001) "Knowing what we know: supporting knowledge creation and sharing in social networks", *Organizational Dynamics*, Vol. 30, No. 2, pp. 100-20.

Derksen, M. et al. (2012) "Social technologies: Cross-disciplinary reflections on technologies in and from the social sciences", *Theory Psychology*, Vol. 22, No. 2,pp. 139-147.

Divol, R., Edelmann, D., Sarrazin, H. (2012) "Demystifying social media", April, Marketing & Sales Practice

Duarte, A. T. (2011) "Privacy and Health System Solution Case", *Conference proceedings Social Technologies '11: ICT for Social transformations,* 17-18 November, 2011, Vilnius-Net.

Forrester Research (2009) "Global IT Market Outlook: 2009". *Cambridge: Forrester Research, Inc.*

De Gennaro T. (2010) "Social Technologies Will Penetrate IT Management Tools", *Cambridge: Forrester Research, Inc.*

Helmer, O. et al. (1966) *Social Technology*. New York, NY: Basic Books

Henderson, C. R. (1895) "Review". *Journal of Political Economy*, Vol. 3 (2), pp. 236-238.

Johannessen, J.A., Olaise, J., Olsen, B. (2001) "Aspects of innovation theory based on knowledge-management", *International Journal of Information Management*, Vol. 19, Iss. 2, pp. 121-139.

Jue A.L, Marr, J.A., Kassatokis, M.E. (2009) *Social media at work: How networking tools propel organizational performance*, John Willey&Sons, NJ, Hoboken

Klososky, S. (2011) "Social Media: Four Ways to Make Social Technologies Relevant to Your Business", *TechNet MAgazin*, access online 16 Sep. 2012, url: http://technet.microsoft.com/en-us/magazine/hh219267.aspx

Koo, Ch. et al. (2011) "Examination of how social aspects moderate the relationship between task characteristics and usage of social communication technologies (SCTs) in organizations", *International Journal of Information Management*, Vol. 31, p. 445-459.

Koplowitz, R. (2010) "Enterprise Social Networking 2010 Market Overview", *Forrester Research.*

Koplowitz R., Owens L. (2010) "Disciplined Social Innovation", *Cambridge: Forrester Research, inc.*

Li, Ch., Bernoff, J. (2012) "Groundswell, Expanded and Revised Edition: Winning in a World Transformed by Social Technologies," Harvard Business School Press Books, pp. 352 .

Leichteris, R. (2011) "Mokslo ir technologijų parkai socialinių technologijų kontekste". *Social Technologies*, Vol. 1(1), pp 139–150.

Mayer, K. (2009) "Who produces social technologies?" access online 16 Sep. 2012, url: http://socialtechnology.wordpress.com/2009/10/23/who-produces-social-technologies/

McKinsey Global Survey (2012) McKinsey Global Survey results, access online 16 Sep. 2012, url: http://www.mckinseyquarterly.com/Business_Technology/BT_Strategy/Minding_your_ digital_business_McKinsey_Global_Survey_results_2975

Nelson, R. R. (2008) "Factors affecting the power of technological paradigms", *Industrial and Corporate Change*, Vol. 17, Number 3, p. 485–497.

North, D., Wallis, J. (1994) "Integrating institutional change and technological change in economic history: a transaction cost approach", *Journal of Institutional and Theoretical Economics*, Vol. 150, p. 609–624.

Rao, M. (2005) *Knowledge Management Tools and Techniques: practitioners and experts evaluate KM solutions*, Burlington (USA): Elsevier Butterworth-Heinemann.

Schotter, A. (1981) *The economic theory of social institutions*. Cambridge: Cambridge University Press.

Schooley C. (2008) "Informal Methods Challenge Corporate Learning", *Cambridge: Forrester Research, inc.*

Small, A. W. (1898) "Seminar Notes: The Methodology of the Social Problem. Division I. The Sources and Uses of Material", *The American Journal of Sociology*, Vol. 4(1), pp. 113-144.

Sproull, L., Faraj, S. (1997) *Atheism, Sex, and Databases: the Net as a Social Technology, in Culture of the Internet*, Mahwah: Lawrence Erlbaum Associates, Inc.

Strathern, M. (2000) *Audit Cultures*, London and New York: Routledge.

Sugden, R. (1989). "Spontaneous order". *Journal of Economic Perspectives,* Vol. 3: p. 85–97.

Wikipedia (Wikipedia, the free Encyclopedia) (2012) Social technology, access online 16 Sep. 2012, url: en.wikipedia.org/wiki/Social_technology#cite_note-1

Zupan, N., Kaše, R., (2007) "The role of HR actors in knowledge networks". *International Journal of Manpower*, Vol. 28 No. 3/4, pp. 243-259.

Innovation, Entrepreneurship and Sustainability: "This is an Idea!"

Cláudia Fernandes and Luís Rocha
CATIM Technological Centre for the Metal Working Industry, Porto, Portugal

Abstract: Innovative and entrepreneurial behaviours are the basis for the creation of sustainable products and processes that preserve energy (and natural) resources. With this paper the authors argue and defend that adopting this principle of sustainability, where the response to actual needs in the present does not compromise the ability of future generations to meet their own needs, should be a pillar in educational systems (either formal or informal) and for industrial practices and manufacturing processes. The empirical part of this paper will be developed according to the case study's approach methodology and grounded on "This is an idea!", an activity encompassed in and out of school which is a hands-on project focused on experience, innovation and entrepreneurship for youngsters. The Technological Center has been running the project for 17 years and it has encompassed more than 9,500 youngsters between the ages of 10 and 17. The project's main objective is to develop a positive vision of the industry, of employment opportunities and technical careers in the industrial sector, towards a sustainable and active citizenship. "This is an idea!"'s activities are designed to allow youngsters to: 1) Give new meanings and interpretations to reality; 2) Rationalise the impact of their learning in real settings; 3) Promote sustainable consumption and production awareness; 4) Develop new ideas promoting innovation and entrepreneurship; 5) Gain skills concerning divergent thought (e.g. creativity techniques) and viability evaluation; 6) Promote awareness of technical careers related to industry; 7) Promote awareness of industrial processes and their links to everyday life; 8) Promote and discuss the development of vocational identity. 3 outputs will be discussed and analysed: i) Ecowaters; ii) Hand-Write and iii) Citriwall. These outputs were thought up, questioned and developed by teams of youngsters according to the project principles. The pedagogical focus of the activities and the rationale for the products design is based not only on know-how (actions) and know-who (networking) but also on know-what (facts), know-why (science) and knowing how it works in real settings (industrial literacy), this is to say that besides the theoretical knowledge, the project gives emphasis to tacit knowledge and skills development on a wider scenario promoting sustainability behaviours anchored on innovation and entrepreneurship in the "new generation".

Keywords: entrepreneurship; innovation; hands-on projects; sustainability; raise youth awareness; industry

1. Introduction

Informal out-of-school education, namely hands-on projects, is a powerful starting point for the preparation of a creative workforce which is able to question and apply principles of innovation and sustainability to everyday life activities (products and processes). But, in order to facilitate sustainable innovation, all segments of society must be educated to understand economic and social connections (Autio, 2003; Seliger and Bilge, 2011; Marmot, 2010; Schaltegger et. al, 2012). A new awareness of the importance of innovations in technology, management, industry and everyday life is fundamental to global economic development, the preservation of life and natural resources, along with the creation of social justice (Marmot, 2010). Innovation occurs when potentials are developed/applied and problems are solved.

According to the Sustainable Products Corporation (2012) sustainable products are characterised by providing environmental, social and economic benefits while protecting public health, welfare and environment through their full commercial cycle - from the extraction of raw materials, design, manufacturing or recycling, among others.

According to the theoretical background and technical expertise, the authors suggest the 3 P matrix analyses for sustainable products/processes: People, Product, and Planet. Each one of the vectors is closely related with the creation of social justice/fairness: People, the social vector, where the impact on lives, groups and society is questioned, and aspects such as quality of life, quality of work and working conditions, education and training, entrepreneurship behaviours are looked upon; Product, the manufacturing vector, where questions about manufacturing and production processes and their impacts are asked; and Planet, the environmental vector, where impacts on finite resources, recycling and re-use, and consumption patterns are looked upon.

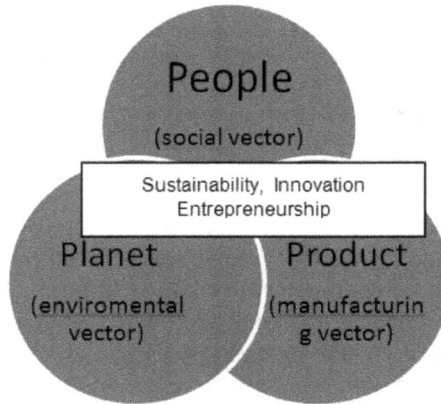

Figure 1: 3 P matrix analyses – People, Product, and Planet

2. Method

This paper is based on the case study methodology. It allows researchers to go to the field and study experiments in their natural setting and context. This methodology is particularly appropriate for "practical-based" problems where the actors' experiences are important, and the phenomenon's context is critical (Benbasat et al, 1987). Multiple sources of evidence were used, e.g. team reports, strategic documents, technical documentation produced by youngsters, analytical reports by the jury and technical staff, project outputs, press news. The paper will be based on qualitative data.

3. This is an idea!

"This is an idea!" (TIAI!) is an activity encompassed within a wider project - "Think Industry Technology" (TIT). TIT is a hands-on, extra-curricular project, tailored for the country's specifications (e.g. Portuguese industrial sectors) based on previously developed and validated intervention models. It encompasses youngsters between the ages of 10 and 17 years old, and it has been running in this technological centre since 1995 (Rocha, 1998) with more than 9,500 youngsters involved in it just in CATIM (Centro de Apoio Tecnológico à Indústria Metalomecânica). The global project encompasses several different stakeholders such as: general citizens, parents, youngsters, the Technological Centres Network, industrial companies, universities, polytechnics and research institutes, industrial and professional bodies, education and training providers, national and local government and government agencies. The project rationale was based on three problem dimensions: i) traditional image from the industry; ii) withdrawal of school children from industrial activities and careers; iii) training choices and market integration heavily influenced by commerce and services. The global aim is to develop a positive vision of the industry and employment opportunities and technical careers in the industrial sector toward an active and sustainable citizenship (see table 1).

Table 1: TIT main problem dimensions specific and global targets (source Fernandes and Rocha, 2001)

Main Problem Dimensions	Specific Targets	
Traditional image of the Industry	• Develop a positive vision of the industry • To link industry with positive values and attractive careers	To develop a positive vision of the industry and of employment opportunities and technical careers in the industrial sector towards an active and sustainable citizenship
Withdrawal of school children from industrial activities and careers	• To make youngsters and industry closer (and vice-versa) • Evolve youngsters and industry in mutual approximation processes	
Training choices and market integration heavily influenced by commerce and services	• Make youngsters aware of industrial careers in short term • Motivate youngsters to carry on their studies in technological areas	

The project has several different activities (see figure 2) that were designed so that youngsters discover alternative sustainable ways of learning, working and living in society – e.g. using Communities of practice (virtual or in-person), e-learning groups (Fernandes and Rocha, 2007; Fernandes and Rocha 2006 a, b; Rocha and Fernandes, 2006), practice teams, simulation games (Fernandes and Rocha, 2011), laboratory activities or field trips.

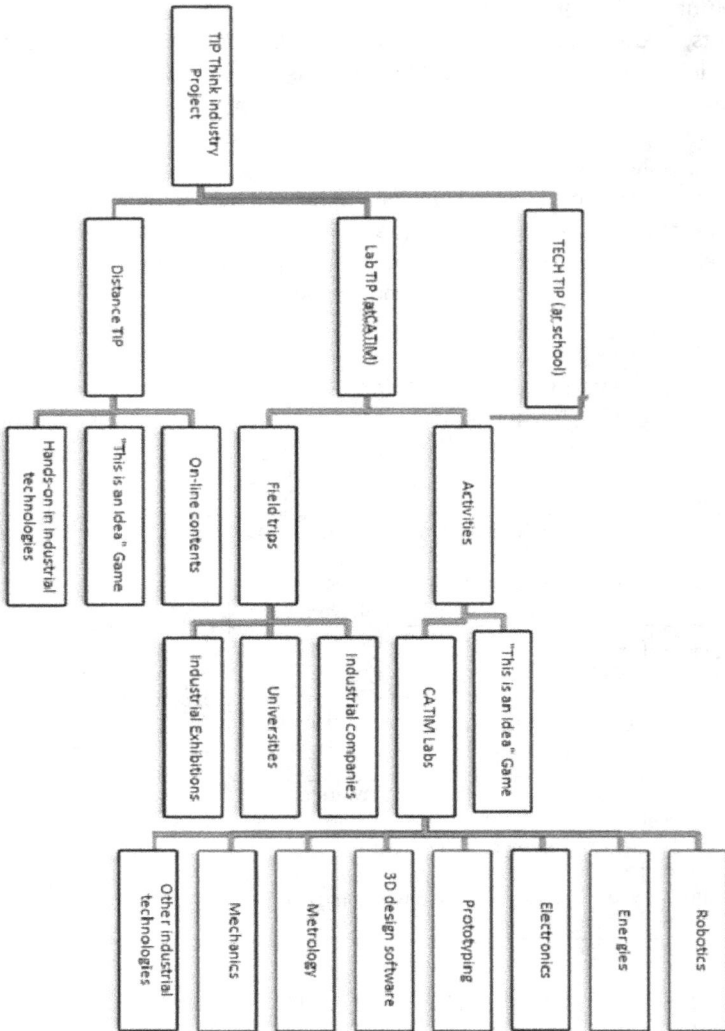

Figure 2: TIT segment activities

On this paper the authors will focus on the activity segment simulation games with "This is an idea!" (Tiai!). Tiai! is a simulation game designed to foster innovative and sustainable thoughts and to promote entrepreneurship and industrial property rights. It's an industrial simulation game to be played in groups. Each team has to come up with an idea for a new product/service/process. This product/service/process must have three criteria so that it can go forward:

- There should not be any similar product/service in the market;

- It should be feasible and sustainable (economic and environmental);

- It should have selling potential.

The next step is the simulation of a constitution of an industrial enterprise. At this point it's necessary to go by every industrial stage, starting from the birth of the "idea" until the product/service is placed on the market. The objective is to understand the product/service industrial cycle and to promote sustainable entrepreneurship and innovation among youngsters. The simulation game has four major phases:

- Team constitution – the groups should have four to six players;

- Role definition - each player will be the chief/manager for a determined business area, with the following areas to distribute: CEO; Selling and Marketing; Innovation and Development; Finance; Production; Human Resources;

- Idea operationalization;

- Prototyping.

The game begins with a "brainstorming" session between all the managers which should take about 30 minutes. All the team members give ideas (no matter how silly they might appear) for the development of the new product/service/process. One idea is chosen based on the commercial potential and on the previous exposed criteria. The product to be developed and produced by the company is hereby defined. Each "manager" must think about several aspects (see figure 2) and the main conclusions are used to operationalize the idea and to fill in the final project form, so that the prototyping can begin!

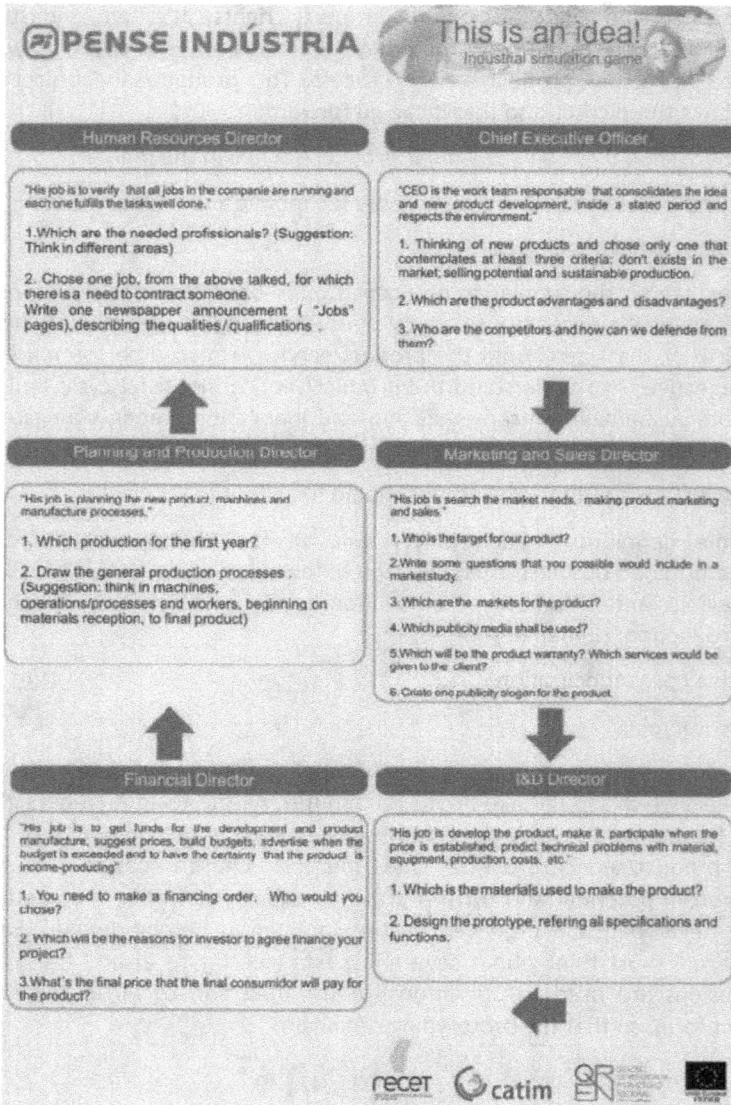

Figure 3: Industrial cycle

The authors will present and discuss the following examples – Ecowaters, Hand-write, Citrowall - that arose from the simulation game Tiai!. All the products presented were registered and the teams own the property rights of them.

3.1. Ecowaters

Ecowaters was an idea developed by a group of four boys between 14 to 15 years old in the Portuguese Formal Teaching System. The team thought about everyday life tasks and got to one driver: "the need of some products that will be sustainable, ecological and profitable". This was the pinpoint when the idea started to take shape. They figured out that when someone wants to take a warm shower, they switch on the hot water tap, and must then wait for the hot water and a lot of "good" water is wasted, so they decided to solve this issue. The challenge was set: "To develop a mechanism that saves the cold water until the hot water comes to our shower". Following these steps, Ecowaters was born, a simple mechanism which re-uses cheap existing parts which allows water to be saved and re-used.

Ecowaters consists of installing a temperature sensor and a valve that allows only hot water (temperature defined by the user) to flow out to the shower. Before this point, it is redirected for later use.

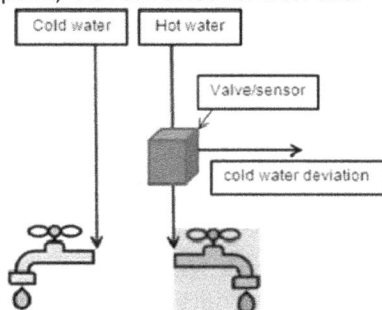

Figure 4: Ecowaters prototype

3.2. Help-Write

Help-Write was an idea developed by a group of five students (4 girls and 1 boy) with ages from 15 to 16 years old, in the Portuguese Formal Teaching System. The team focused on everyday life tasks: "some tasks seem very simple, but for some people, such as those with different motion capabilities, they get very complicated". This was the point at which the idea started to take shape. In regular classes the team had a school colleague with a physical problem. He could not use a pen or a pencil as most of us do and "fine motor" movements are hard for him to perform due to a physical handicap. This was the problem situation they decided to solve.

So a question was set: "Why can't we develop a mechanism that helps people pick a pen up in such a way that people with low fine motor skills can experience the pleasure of drawing or writing?". Following these steps Help-Write was born, a simple, cheap, easy-to-handle mechanism that helps the user to hold a pen/pencil, and at the same time move the hands and have better movement control. Help-Write is an ergonomic support device that adapts to the hand where a pen can be settled. It contains a wristband so that the frustration of letting objects fall can be avoided (see figure 5).

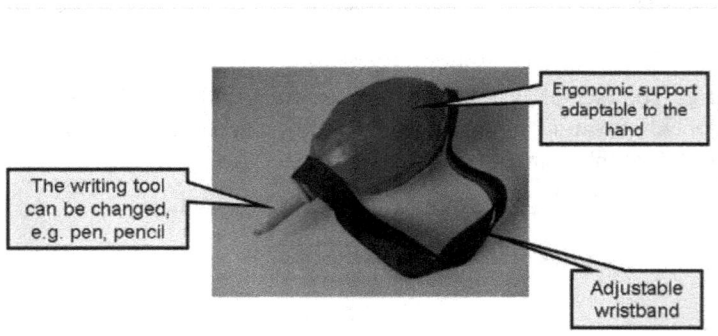

Figure 5: Help-Write prototype

The use of "Help-Write" can be generalised for various other situations, e.g. recovery from vascular diseases, hand exercise for older people, help people with temporary mobility difficulties to write. This idea was the winner of the 2007 national contest and it has been registered in the National Institute for Intellectual Property.

3.3. Citriwall

Citriwall was an idea developed by a team of 3 boys with ages from 16 to 17 that were on the Portuguese Technical Teaching System. The idea arose due to the life experiences from the team members – a technical teaching system and personal hobbies such as product design and ceramics.

Figure 6: Citriwall prototype

Citriwall was designed to be put on kitchen walls performing three functions: squeezing oranges, making the area more pleasant, and contributing to water saving.

4. Discussion

Tiai! was not designed to achieve "scientific literacy" but to promote "industrial literacy", even though it is based on scientific and engineering principles. By industrial literacy we mean to promote knowledge on several aspects from the industry: industrial product/service life-cycle, advanced manufacturing technologies, sustainable products/processes, general theoretical and practical principles and implications, Industrial Property rights, the perception of industry, etc. But Tiai! activities are also designed to deal with specific objectives of developing innovation, creativity, sustainability and entrepreneurial spirit among youngsters. Analysing the simulation game, the idea generation process was very fruitful for every team: lots of ideas arose, but most of them already existed, e.g. a microwave with a TV receiver, a chewing-gum disposal bucket, a pair of tennis shoes that grow with the feet. Only when the youngsters started to think about their own everyday lives and experiences did ideas start to take shape and be operationalized. The conjunction of content knowledge, process skills knowledge and sustainable entrepreneurship awareness made the presented products possible – Ecowaters, Help-Write and Citriwall. Youngsters become aware that their knowledge is not confined by formal teaching and contents of a curriculum; their context and experiences are added value for what they can do in the present and in the future in several aspects of their lives (e.g. private, professional).

Table 2: 3 P Matrix applied to Tiai! products (Ecowaters, Hand-write, Citriwall)

	People Social vector	Product Manufacturing vector	Planet Environmental vector
Ecowaters	Entrepreneurship Incremental innovation Peer recognition Stakeholders recognition	Re-use ofavailable resources (products, and sub-products) Incremental production	Reduce waste water Re-use water Rational use of natural resources Re-use of components Environmental conscience
Hand-write	Entrepreneurship Incremental innovation Peer recognition Stakeholders recognition Social conscience Fairness for all	Re-use ofavailable resources (products, and sub-products) Incremental production	Rational use of resources Re-use of components
Citriwall	Entrepreneurship Radical innovation Peer recognition Stakeholders recognition	Design innovation Functionality New 3D prototyping technology Manufacturing conscience	Rational use of resources Re-use of components in different ways (composite material)

The authors suggest that sustainable innovations via entrepreneurism can be accessed by the 3 P matrix: People (Social vector), Product (Manufacturing vector) and Planet (Environmental vector). The analysis matrix was applied to the Tiai! products Ecowaters, Hand-write and Citriwall. Please see table 2.

We can clearly notice that prior to Tiai! Activities, youngsters have generic and imprecise images of the product cycle, industrial processes and predictions concerning sustainability of new (or renewed) products, while after participating in Tiai! Activities, youngsters start to change their global perceptions on industry and industrial careers along with an increased awareness of sustainable entrepreneurial issues. The connection of their actions and possible consequences on people, product and planet is clearer. With Tiai! and its outputs (e.g. Helpwrite, Ecowaters, Citriwall) we can see that innovation, big breakthroughs, and entrepreneurship appear anywhere, with people of any age! Entrepreneurship/ innovative spirit and sustainable behaviours can be incited. Intellectual creativity and "different ways" of seeing the same reality are important assets for the development of entrepreneurial capabilities.

5. Conclusions

Industry, namely manufacturing, has huge potential for generating wealth, jobs, better quality of life and for promoting a fair and just society. This "new" industry must compete by adding value to the processes and products, and not just by reducing costs. These assets are made possible by the promotion of innovation and entrepreneurship with the help of trained and skilful people. Industry must attract and hold on to capable and qualified people going beyond demographic trends of aging and the unattractiveness of industry/manufacturing as a career. Solutions must encompass all areas, including formal and informal education, life-long learning, and the promotion of healthier workplaces among many others. New reindustrialisation is required in most countries in order to face these other new or emerging challenges.

Entrepreneurship can be encouraged and promoted from young ages in a variety of forms, from out-of-school activities (e.g. the TIAI simulation game and other TIT activities), to the design of curricula, approaches to teaching, government policies and programs, sectorial associations' intervention programs and campaigns, and many others. There are contexts that facilitate entrepreneurship, such as environments that are open to new ideas and where there is freedom to research and solve problems; there are times when these assets are not present in most public and private schools. It is also important to make youngsters aware of their capabilities and power to innovate and to be entrepreneurs contributing to a better and fairer society. Contexts which are open to entrepreneurship and innovation must also deal with failure; good ideas are not always big breakthroughs. On the other hand, there are also environments which inhibit entrepreneurship and innovation, e.g. places or schools with excessive rules/procedures and control, and are not open to new ideas/activities. Young entrepreneurs (and others of all ages) need to have a keen eye to understand economic, social, and scientific realities and the capacity to understand evolutionary processes in the future. In other words they must have the capability to "see the big picture".

Scientific data, common sense and intuition have told us that there is much to be done in the fields of innovation, sustainability and entrepreneurship to achieve economic growth along with a sustainable, prosperous and fair society. The Government, business people and researchers are aware and are taking action. But programs like TIT and activities like TIAI! show that everybody has the power to act. Youngsters have an immense innovative and entrepreneurial potential that must be encouraged and fostered so that an entrepreneurial and innovative culture is made possible, and that we can aim towards a fair society.

6. Acknowledgements

Portuguese and European Founds (QREN – COMPETE – FEDER) grants finance Think Industry
Project (01/SIAC/2008, project number 5248). This project is promoted by RECET.

References

Autio, E. (1993)Technology transfer effects of new, technology-based companies: an empirical study,
Helsinki University of Technology/Institute of Industrial Management, Helsinki.
Benbasat, I., Goldstein, D. and Mead, M. (1987) "The Case Study Research Strategy in Information
Systems" MIS Quarterly, Vol. 11, No. 3, pp 396-386.
Fernandes, C. and Rocha, L (2006) The Conceptualization and Analyses of a Value Network: How to
Create Value with Inter Organizational Communities of Practice? In José Cordeiro, Vitor Pedrosa,
Bruno Encarnação and Joaquim Filipe (Eds), Proceedings on Society, e-Business, e-Government and e-Learning for the Second International Conference on Web Information Systems and Technologies, INSTICC – Institute for Systems and Technologies of Information, Control and Communication, Setúbal.
Fernandes, C. and Rocha, L. (2006) Value Networks the Source of Collective Community Intelligence: One Case Study. In Piet Kommers, Pedro Isaías and Ambrosio Oikoetxea (Eds), Process of the International Association for Development of the Information Society – Web Based Communities

2006, IADIS, San Sebastian.

Fernandes, C. and Rocha, L. (2007). Pedagogy for collaborative learning: Technological and human issues in Proceedings of the IADIS International Conference on Web Based Communities 2007, IADIS, Salamanca.

Fernandes, C. and Rocha, L. (2011). Manufacturing Sustainability: Aligning youth mindsets. In Selinger, G, Khraisheh, M., Jawahir, I. (eds). Advances in Sustainable Manufacturing. New York, CIRP/Springer.

Rocha, L. (1998). Promover a Inovação e o Empreendorismo Junto dos Jovens Pense Indústria Inovação. In Motor de Innovación Ponencias y Comunicaciones Presentadas en el V Congreso Galego da Calidade, Xunta de Galicia, Santiago de Compostela.

Schaltegger, S., Laddeke–Freund, F., Hansen, E. (2012) "Business cases for sustainability: the role of business model innovation for corporate sustainability", International Journal of Innovation and Sustainable Development , Vol. 6(2) 95-119.

Seliger, G., Reise, C., and Bilge, P. (2011). Curriculum design for sustainable engineering – Experiences from the international master program "Global production engineering". In Selinger, G, Khraisheh, M., Jawahir, I. (eds). Advances in Sustainable Manufacturing, CIRP/Springer, New York. Sustainable Products Corporation (2012). What are sustainable products? [On-line] Sustainable Products Corporation, http://www.sustainableproducts.com/susproddef.html.

Business Modelling for Sustainability: Identifying Five Modelling Principles and Demonstrating their Role and Function in an Explorative Case Study

Jan Jonker[1] and Nikolay Dentchev[2]
[1]Nijmegen School of Management (NSM),Radboud University Nijmegen (RU), Holland
[2]University of Brussels (VUB) and HUBrussel, Belgium

Abstract: The mainstream literature describes businesses as tools for earning money (e.g. Osterwalder, 2004, Magretta, 2002). Although profit generation is an important business outcome, it tends to overlook the business opportunity in embracing issues of sustainability. Conventional business models theories do not capture the value of social and environmental assets, nor do they stimulate the development of business models focused on the solution of sustainability issues (i.e. not on earning money). We approach this void in the literature from the perspective of sustainability and corporate social responsibility. Literature on this topic was used a top-down theorizing approach (Shepherd and Sutcliffe, 2011) that allowed us to propose 5 additional principles of business modelling next to the principle of profitability: (1) multiple value creation; (2) basic logic; (3) strategic choice; (4) value network and (5) cooperative organizing. We have provided further corroborative evidence of these principles from an explorative case study of Close the Gap. This paper extends the profit generation focus in the literature of business planning toward principles of sustainability. Attention to social and environmental issues makes perfect sense in business, and can lead to new opportunities.

Keywords: sustainable business models, sustainable development, corporate social responsibility, profit generation, case study, theory building

1. Introduction

Conventional business models are predominantly oriented towards shaping the process of making money. Osterwalder argues that, "A business model is a conceptual tool that contains a set of elements and their relationships and allows expressing a *company's logic of earning money.*"(Osterwalder, 2004) p. 15, emphasis added). Using Magretta (2002), business models can be described as narrative and exactable stories, in which human behaviour and stakeholder motivations are combined in such a way that makes sense. This may initially appear to be a different approach to business modelling, however, she then subsequently stresses that business models answer one of "the fundamental questions every manager must ask: How do we make money in this business?" (Magretta, 2002), p. 87). This perspective on business models significantly resembles mainstream neo-classical economic thinking. A famous proponent of this theory, Milton Friedman, once asserted that the only social responsibility of business organizations is profit generation (Friedman, 1970). Although earning money and profit generation are important business derivatives, this paper intends to question the centrality of this thinking by exploring how sustainability can be embedded into business models.

Traditionally, business models are not (always) oriented towards the values and principles of sustainable development, perhaps due to the fact that these are not expressed in monetary terms. Excluding these values and principles from business models is a clear shortcoming, in view of the challenges that our planet is facing. Even businessmen, exposed to the pressure of profit generation, acknowledge that business models are about more than earning money. Herman Wijffels (former CEO of the Dutch Rabobank), for example, asserts that "What companies do isn't just important to shareholders and employees, but also to society and the earth as the source of life as well" (Wijffels, 1999, p. 113). We readily acknowledge that many businessmen, even amongst the most hardnosed and profit-driven, are convinced of the need for sustainability. Their attention is caught by the "Inconvenient Truth", as Al Gore would say. In other words, the attention of businessmen is caught once the risks of global warming, resource depletion, and social instability for their businesses become evident. Without doubt, some business leaders pay genuinely personal attention to sustainability; however, their numbers must be rather insignificant, as evidenced by Ban Ki-moon, the secretary-general of the United Nations, recently stating that our current model of economic development and growth is 'suicidal' (Source: digital press-release website World Economic Forum, Davos, 2011).

Since conventional business models pay insufficient attention to sustainability, this void will be addressed here. This paper first elaborates on the values and principles of sustainability and subsequently, illustrates them in an exploratory case study. This pattern allows the paper to strengthen theory building of sustainable business models. An empirical example of a successful sustainable business model is also provided in support of our theory that there are powerful alternatives to resolve the sustainability issues of our planet. We conclude this contribution with a discussion on the implication of our ideas on sustainability management and on future research.

2. Sustainability principles

The literature on sustainable development has a long tradition of opposition to emphasising on profit generation alone. The contemporary idea of sustainable development is concerned with addressing social capital and protecting the natural environment in addition to creating welfare (Aguirre, 2002). This central idea refers to the so-called triple bottom line principle advanced by Elkington (1997). According to this principle, companies should organise themselves in such a way that they pay simultaneous attention to people, planet and profit. Waddock goes one step further and is even a proponent of multiple-bottom lines (Waddock, 2000). Extending the profit bottom line, as argued by the World Commission for Sustainable Development, needs to take place "in harmony and enhance both current and future potential to meet human needs and aspirations" (Brundtland, 1987), p. 46). In other words, our attention to multiple bottom lines needs to also be sustained over time with attention paid to future generations.

Related perspectives on sustainable development (e.g., corporate social responsibility, social return on investment, and circular economy) are opposed to the neo-classical dogma of 'pure' profit generation(Windsor, 2001, Wood, 2000, Margolis and Walsh, 2003, Dentchev, 2009). Carroll adds to the economic principle of profit generation three principles of corporate social responsibility: legal, ethical and discretionary (Carroll, 1979, Carroll, 1991). Business organizations are expected, in the CSR tradition, to prevent negative social impacts and to promote social prosperity (Fitch, 1976, Jones et al., 2000, Wells, 1998). Overall, corporate social responsibility advances normatively correct principles of business (Swanson, 1995, Wartick and Cochran, 1985, Wood, 1991). CSR scholars have even attempted to demonstrate the superiority of their theory over the neo-classical economic theory by demonstrating that CSR leads to superior financial performance (Orlitzky et al., 2003). However, such a demonstration proves quite challenging due to the high level of aggregation and the complexity of the phenomena under study (Jawahar and McLaughlin, 2001, Griffin and Mahon, 1997, Arlow and Gannon, 1982, Margolis and Walsh, 2001). As these studies revealed positive, neutral, and negative relationships between CSR and financial performance, certain scholars have argued in favour of more corroborative approaches to CSR strategies (Dentchev, 2004, Perrini et al., 2011). Taking into account the inability of many organisations to address organizing multiple values competence development in this respect is urgently needed. Evidently this will take time. Addressing these matters may not be the quickest path to wealth, however, it is a very appropriate way to solve pressing social and environmental issues involving our planet.

In addition to the idea of multiple bottom lines, sustainable development scholars argue in favour of inclusive and connected development (Gladwin et al., 1995). This implies the attention and involvement of stakeholders including the less privileged (Sen et al., 2002). It also implies that businesses engage not only the most powerful stakeholders (in terms of the capability of being heard and exercising influence) (Clarkson, 1995) but also those on the fringe(Hart and Sharma, 2004). The engagement of these stakeholders results, ultimately, in positive business outcomes, since these groups are powerful sources of innovation and an important source for future businesses.

In terms of business models, the above principles of sustainability imply simultaneous attention to the business case, the natural case, and the social case (Birkin et al., 2009). In other words, sustainable business models possess the ability to generate multiple values. Engagement with a wide range of fringe stakeholders, as Hart and Sharma (2004) demonstrate, is based on clear business logic. They contribute to sustaining the operating business while opening up new horizons and innovative opportunities for the organization. In addition, Prahalad (2010) clearly indicates that attention to the "bottom of the pyramid" is a sound strategic choice rather than an idealistic decision. The same strategic logic is argued for companies with proactive attention to environmental issues (Buysse and Verbeke, 2003, Aragón-Correa and Sharma, 2003).

Integrating sustainability in business models requires a systemic and holistic approach (Senge et al., 2008, Dentchev et al., 2011). From this perspective, multiple value creation is realized as a joint effort between the organization and its stakeholders. It is the culmination of stakeholder engagement and cooperation in an environment that enables such cooperation (Simanis and Hart, 2009). Sustainable business models are based on the conception that value networks of stakeholders create value in cooperation. These networks share a basic logic – a set of values – and have made a strategic choice regarding the issues they will address in their collective organizational efforts. Based on the above, a number of principles enabling the creation of sustainable business models can be identified: (1) multiple value creation; (2) basic logic; (3) strategic choice; (4) value network and (5) cooperative organizing.

3. An explorative case study

We would like to illustrate the above principles of sustainable business models in a corroborative case study. The development of this case study follows an inductive top-down theorizing approach (Shepherd and Sutcliffe, 2011). According to Shepherd and Sutcliffe:

"Inductive top-down theorizing begins with data contained in the literature from which problems (tensions, conflicts, and/or contradictions) and potential solutions (literature, theories, constructs, relationships) emerge to offer a description and then a coherent resolution of a research problem, ultimately constituting a new theory of organization." (p. 366)

In fact, the preceding sections of this paper were based on literature where we have identified the tension between the conventional business models theory (advancing profit generation) and sustainability (advancing attention to multiple values and multiple stakeholders). As a result, we proposed five fundamentals of sustainable business models (multiple value creation, basic logic, strategic choice, value network, cooperative organizing) and would like to corroborate them with an exploratory case study.

We have studied the case of Close the Gap, a non-profit organization active in IT systems for low budget projects primarily in developing countries, and headquartered in Brussels, Belgium. This case was selected due to its fit with the phenomenon of our study, sustainable business models, and on the following criteria: (i) profit generation is not central (non-profit); (ii) attention is given to social issue (IT access in developing countries); (iii) attention is given to environmental issues (recycling of IT systems); and (iv) the success of the initiative (UN recognition). The second author conducted a systematic search in a Belgian newspaper database, Mediargus (on 13.03.2013) and gathered 57 pages (A4, Times New Roman font, single spacing) of articles about Close the Gap.

The article publication dates range from 3.4.2003 to 3.10.2012. Our search resulted in 115 articles. After eliminating irrelevant articles and the same article being published in different journals, we gathered information from 48 articles. The articles are in Dutch and further quotations in this text are free translations. In addition, this information was triangulated with the organization's website (http://www.close-the-gap.org), annual reports, a film describing the organization (duration 12:12 min), and the testimony of its founder, Olivier van den Eynde, during the second author's class time on 27.11.2012 (duration 1h30min).

4. 'Close the Gap International' and its sustainable business model

4.1. Background

Olivier van den Eynde (b.1979) founded Close the Gap International vzw (hereafter, Close the Gap) in 2003 during his studies at the University of Brussels (VUB), Belgium. The initiative began as a student enterprise of a group of six students during his studies in commercial engineering. Olivier's idea was a natural result of his father's decision to renew the computers at his company. Olivier, the oldest in a family of 6 children, recycled the old computers into an IT network for his siblings. This led to the epiphany, "If an SME like my father's replaces PC's like that every few years, what about multinationals?" Olivier realized that an old PC can easily function for many years after being replaced and could be more beneficial in developing countries, where resources for IT are a luxury. Hence, this straight-forward logic gave birth to Close the Gap, i.e., closing the digital gap in developing countries. Following his studies, Olivier dedicated himself full time to developing this noble venture and even rejected two career proposals within the big 4 consultant firms. Ten years later, Close the Gap has been recognized as a UN – NGO with 250.000 donated PCs realised in projects in 40 countries.

4.2. Basic logic

Close the Gap approaches the social issue of digital exclusion with a basic, simple logic. Quoted in an article in Het Nieuwsblad dd 26.11.2013, Olivier vanden Eynde explains this logic as follows: "Companies change their computers every 3 to 4 years while there is, basically, nothing wrong with these computers. Removing them safely costs easily 50 EUR per computer, so we offer an alternative: we collect the computers and take care of all necessary treatments and logistics". Hence, old computers function perfectly in such a second life and could be beneficial in budget sensitive communities. Close the Gap guarantees the certified elimination of the information from the computers. Subsequently, they repair and clean the computers, install new software, and ship them to developing countries.

The same basic and simple logic was applied when Close the Gap derived a spin-off activity known as WorldLoop. The service performed by WorldLoop is oriented to recycling outdated PCs in developing countries. Close the Gap realized that, by solving one sustainability issue (closing the digital gap in budget limited environments), another was fuelled, i.e. IT waste in developing countries. Hence, WorldLoop organizes the recycling of IT waste in developing countries. For complex recycling matters, which could not be resolved locally, the organization discovered a solution in the Umicore n.v. plant near Antwerp, becoming one of the few organizations authorized to import industrial garbage into Belgium.

4.3. Value network

During the 10 year journey of Close the Gap, it depended on a profound and valuable network. Advice and active support was granted by Nobel Prize Winner Desmond Tutu; King Philippe and Queen Mathilde of Belgium; IOC chairman Jacques Rogge; (former) European Commissioners Neelie Kroes, Étienne Davignon and Karel Van Miert; (former) ministers Frank Vandenbroucke, Xavier de Donnea, Louis Michel and Patricia

Ceysens; along with many professors, businessmen and friends. Such an extended network adds value to the project and stimulates commitment, contacts, and further opportunities for growth.

A good example of active support exists in initiatives that have attracted media attention and sponsoring. For example, Professor Wim Blonk (VUB), former director of the European Commission, supported Close the Gap with a remarkable initiative. He completed a cycling tour in May 2003 of 4.000 kilometres in France and generated some publicity and sponsoring. This type of publicity and sponsoring effort was repeated in 2007 by two proponents in their mid-20s, Luk De Brauwer and Alex Gay, who accepted the challenge of a 9.200 km touring in Africa with a Citroen 2 PK.In June 2012, another initiative called "Bike to Close the Gap", gathered more than 200 cyclists, 55.000 EUR sponsoring, and the needed media attention. Overall, such initiatives further fuel the value network and attract the attention of potentially valuable stakeholders.

4.4. Cooperative organizing

Close the Gap began, in its infancy, with limited forces and without profit. Even currently (i.e. December 2011, last available financial figures) the organization counted 3,8 FTEs despite the extended activity and positive financials, cf. 4,7 million EUR cash on balance (or ca. 84 % of the total balance sheet). The ability to obtain 250.000 donated computers and to realize projects in 40 countries with such a limited force is only possible in a model of cooperative organizing. The following "cooperative" partners seem to be crucial for Close the Gap:

- Donation: There are dozens of well-known companies ready to donate. Close the Gap works with business partners (not private) to realize economies of scale. Additionally, the donating companies are also occasionally involved in the advertisement and the realisation of the projects.

- Refurbishment: Flection Group (http://www.flection.com) removes data from old computers, repairs them, and installs new software. The Windows software license is almost free with the guarantee that computers are employed in non-commercial projects.

- Project selection: Local authorities, local NGO's, and the UN provide a solid base for selecting promising projects. Close the Gap works predominantly with social projects, universities, hospitals, and NGO's and avoids individual and commercial projects.

- Installation, training and maintenance: Projects are accomplished by local social entrepreneurs who realize the installation, training (partially), and maintenance.

- Transport: KLM Cargo transports for free, shows Close the Gap films to passengers, and motivates them to exchange miles in support of the project. One of the first transportations of PCs was shipped to Congo in the airplane of the foreign minister at the time, Louis Michel.

- Recycling: Recupel and Umicor are partners in the recycling process. Both are experts in this field.

4.5. Strategic choice

On many occasions, the above-mentioned partners, utilizing cooperative organizing, have made strategic choices which led to their involvement in Close the Gap. For example, the companies donating computers do so for philanthropic reasons that enhance their reputation (Dentchev, 2004, Fombrun et al., 2000, Fombrun, 2001). Concurrently, these donors are concerned with cost efficiency and the safe removal of information from their computers. In a newspaper article in De Tijd, Jozef Schildemans and Johan Zwiekhorst (dd 17.11.2004) explain that simple formatting of PC disks (and other digital devices) does not sufficiently, nor safely, remove all information. According to this article, it is more advantageous for companies to outsource this activity to specialized service providers for economic reasons; the safe removal of information appears rather time consuming. Close the Gap guarantees a certified removal of information. This task is outsourced to Flection in Kontich, Belgium, an ISO 9002 certified company, who subsequently prepare the computers for their second life. Close the Gap even provides a professional solution for their donors by allowing a savings of approximately 50 EUR with the removal of old computers and the corporate information contained in them. Safe removal of corporate information is not only of economic value. We believe that it is a key element in the success of Close the Gap's sustainable business model, as donating companies are sensitive to possible leaks of (sometimes) secret corporate information. Cumulatively, all partners in the cooperative network have a strategic reason for joining forces with Close the Gap.

Yet, Close the Gap has also made sound strategic choices. It remains headquartered at the University of Brussels (VUB) campus with the legal status of a not-for-profit organization. An idealistic and enthusiastic student can count on the support of many, as mentioned above. We suspect, however, that this project would not have been so successful in a for-profit oriented initiative, or as a hobby of an established manager. The idealism and attention to quality attracts the support of many, and the manner in which this sustainable business model is structured indicates genuine quality.

4.6. Multiple value creation

Close the Gap does not freely give away the computers but sells them for c. 50 EUR to cover all expenses and logistics. Selling them, instead of giving them away, also guarantees the involvement of local parties. Additionally, these local NGO's and institutions are carefully selected with the advice of Bishop Desmond Tutu. Close the Gap is searching for partners that have the capability to bring the project to success and, of course, would support and coach them throughout its course. In this scenario, not only are the computers valuable, but they provide also the ability for local schools, hospitals, NGO's and government's access to plenty of digital information. Benefit also comes through local repair services, if and when necessary, and the teaching of local users (young and old, with or without disability) to work with computers and with the Internet. In this respect, computers are the necessary condition for the creation of an entire ecosystem that closes the digital gap in developing countries, and which is most valuable in this business model.

It is important to mention here that "value" is most probably perceived differently by each stakeholder. Donors value certified information removal and their contribution to a good cause. Commercial flight carriers value their contribution to local communities, which could be a strategic asset in a regulated business with growing market potential. Local organizations value the overall end-to-end support required for the successful completion of projects. Ultimately, the value created by Close the Gap is social (combating digital exclusion, enhancing human capital), environmental (trough recycling initiatives), and economic (efficiency and effectiveness of local communities).

5. Conclusions

This paper advanced five principles of sustainable business models, specifically, multiple value creation, basic logic, strategic choice, value network and cooperative organizing. These principles were introduced to extend the conventional business model logic, based on pure financial profit generation. We employed an inductive approach to develop these five principles of sustainable business models. An explorative case study of 'Close the Gap' was introduced to corroborate our ideas. This complex case illustrates that sustainable business models can be perfectly grounded in not-for-profit organizations that provide valuable solutions to the multitude of social and environmental issues facing our planet.

Our argument opens up the discussion around business model theorizing on at least on four different levels:

- Sustainability principles in business models: The case of Close the Gap shows how an NGO can be managed according to a mixture of sound business and sustainability principles. However, these principles need further validation. Besides, further research is needed to explore how for profit business organizations put profitability on the background and focus primarily on the principles of sustainability.

- Business models without a profit focus: In this paper, we have challenged the idea that business models are tools for earning money (Osterwalder, 2004, Magretta, 2002). Close the Gap's focus is to close the digital gap in developing countries. Facebook's focus was on building a social network. Google's focus was to organize the world's information. Profit generation is only the result of a business activity, and it would be surprising if all great entrepreneurs were ex ante focusing on the monetary success they have eventually realized. Besides, there are many who focused on the same business opportunities as Zuckerberg, Peage and Brin, but yet did not have the same success (Ries, 2011). Hence, it is even questionable if only one principle is the object focus for entrepreneurs who realize successful ventures.

- Various measures of success: The above discussion raises the possibility that business models can be evaluated upon various measures of success. Could a loss making business model be called successful, and under what conditions?

- Additional variety of legal structures: Close the Gap suggests that an non-profit organization can be extremely liquid (cf. 4,7 mio EUR on balance), i.e. it was profitable. Yet, its legal structure does not provide the opportunity of IPO, selling shares, or merging with other organizations, all of which may have an industrial logic to better address the digital gap in developing countries. Inversely, for-profit organizations that address social and environmental issues may not benefit from a wide support of politicians or opinion makers, who may fear that the ultimate goal behind such noble intentions is profit generation. It hence seems plausible to have hybrid legal structures, or to allow a group of legal structures to comprise a mixture of profit and non-for-profit organizations.

Further research is required in order to address the matters advanced in the above discussion. In any case, more studies are necessary to understand how cohesive the identified principles are, what the transferability of these principles may be to other sectors, and, ultimately, how this may be translated into a new generation of business models.

References

Aguirre, B. E. (2002) "Sustainable development as collective surge", *Social Science Quarterly,* Vol. 83, No.1, pp. 101-118.
Aragón-Correa, J. A. and Sharma, S. (2003) "A contingent resource-based view of proactive corporate environmental strategy", *Academy of Management Review,Vol.* 28, No. 1, pp. 71-88.
Arlow, P. and Gannon, M. J. (1982). "Social responsiveness, corporate structure, and economic performance". *Academy of Management Review,* Vol. 7, No. 2, pp. 235-341.
Birkin, F., Cashman, A., Koh, S. C. L. and Liu, Z. (2009) "New Sustainable Business Models in China", *Business Strategy and the Environment,* Vol. 18, pp. 64-77.
Brundtland, C. H. (1987) *Our common future,* Oxford, Oxford University Press.
Buysse, K. and Verbeke, A. (2003) "Proactive environmental strategies: A stakeholder perspective", *Strategic Management Journal,* Vol. 24, No. 5, pp. 453-470.
Carroll, A. B. (1979) "A three-dimensional conceptual model of corporate performance",. *Academy of Management Review,* Vol. 4, No. 4, pp. 497-505.
Carroll, A. B. (1991) "The pyramid of corporate social responsibility: Toward the moral management of organizational stakeholders", *Business Horizons,* Vol. 34, No. 4, pp. 39-48.

Clarkson, M. B. E. (1995) "A stakeholder framework for analyzing and evaluating corporate social performance", *Academy of Management Review,* Vol. 20, No. 1, pp. 92-117.

Dentchev, N. A. (2004) "Corporate social performance as a business strategy", *Journal of Business Ethics,* Vol. 55, No. 4, pp. 395-410.

Dentchev, N. A. (2009) "To What Extent Is Business and Society Literature Idealistic?" *Business & Society,* Vol. 48, No. 1, pp. 10-38.

Dentchev, N. A., Heene, A. and Gosselin, D. P. (2011) Integrating corporate social responsibility in business models. *In:* Von Der Oelsnitz, D. and Güttel, W. (eds.) *Jahrbuch Strategisches Kompetenz-Management Band 5: Kooperationsorientierte Kompetenzen.* München: Rainer Hampp Verlag.

Fitch, H. G. (1976) "Achieving corporate social responsibility", *Academy of Management Review,* Vol. 1, No. 1, pp. 38-46.

Fombrun, C. J. (2001) Corporate reputation as economic asset. *In:* Hitt, M. A., Freeman, E. R. & Harrison, J. S. (eds.) *The Blackwell Handbook of Strategic Management.* Oxford: Blackwell Publishers.

Fombrun, C. J., Gardberg, N. A. and Barnett, M. L. (2000) "Opportunity platforms and safety nets: Corporate citizenship and reputational risk", *Business and Society Review,* Vol. 105, No. 1, pp. 85-106.

Friedman, M. (1970) "A Friedman doctrine: The social responsibility of business is to increase its profits", *New York Times Magazine.*

Gladwin, T. N., Kennelly, J. J. and Krause, T.-S. (1995) "Shifting paradigms for sustainable development: Implications for management theory and research", *Academy of Management Review,* Vol. 20, No. 4, pp. 874-907.

Griffin, J. J. and Mahon, J. F. (1997) "The corporate social performance and corporate financial performance debate: Twenty-five years of incomparable research", *Business & Society,* Vol. 36, No. 1, pp. 5-31.

Hart, S. L. and Sharma, S. (2004) "Engaging fringe stakeholders for competitive imagination", *Academy of Management Executive,* Vol. 18, No. 1, pp. 7-18.

Jawahar, I. M. and McLaughlin, G. L. (2001) "Toward a descriptive stakeholder theory: An organizational life cycle approach", *Academy of Management Review,* Vol. 26, No. 3, pp. 397-414.

Jones, G. R., George, J. M. and Hill, C. W. L. (2000) *Contemporary management,* New York, McGraw-Hill.

Magretta, J. (2002) "Why business models matter", *Harvard Business Review,* Vol. 80, No. 5, pp. 86-91.

Margolis, J. D. and Walsh, J. P. (2001) *People and profits? The search for a link between company's social and financial performance.,* New Jersey, Mahwah.

Margolis, J. D. and Walsh, J. P (2003) "Misery loves companies: Rethinking social initiatives by business", *Administrative Science Quarterly,* Vol. 48, No. 2, pp. 268-305.

Orlitzky, M., Schmidt, F. L. and Rynes, S. L. (2003) "Corporate social and financial performance: A meta-analysis", *Organization Studies,* Vol. 24, No. 3, pp. 403-441.

Osterwalder, A. (2004) *The business model ontology: A proposition in a design science approach* Ph.D Dissertation, University of Lausanne.

Perrini, F., Russo, A., Tencati, A. and Vurro, C. (2011) "Deconstructing the relationship between corporate social and financial performance", *Journal of Business Ethics,* Vol. 102, No. 1, pp. 59 -76.

Ries, E. (2011) The lean startup, Crown Business, New York.

Sen, A., Brundtland, C. H. and Johnson, I. (2002) "Sustainable development". *New Perspectives Quarterly,* Vol. 19, No. 4, pp. 78-83.

Senge, P., Smith, B., Kruschwitz, N., Laur, J. and Schley, S. (2008) *The Necessary Revolution,* Boston, Nicholas Brealey Publishing.

Shepherd, D. A. and Sutcliffe, K. M. (2011) "Inductive Top-Down Theorizing: A Source of New Theories of Organization", *Academy of Management Review,* Vol. 36, Vol. 2, pp. 361-380.

Simanis, E. and Hart, S. (2009) "Innovation From The Inside Out", *MIT Sloan management review,* Vol. 50, No. 4, pp 77-86.

Swanson, D. L. (1995) "Addressing a theoretical problem by reorienting the corporate social performance model", *Academy of Management Review,* Vol. 20, No. 1, pp. 43-64.

Waddock, S. A. (2000) "The multiple bottom lines of corporate citizenship: Social investing, reputation, and responsibility audits", *Business and Society Review,* Vol. 105, No. 3, pp. 323-345.

Wartick, S. L. and Cochran, P. L. (1985) "The evolution of the corporate social performance model", *Academy of Management Review,* Vol. 10, No. 4, pp. 758-769.

Wells, C. (1998) Corporate responsibility. *Encyclopedia of Applied Ethics,* 1.

Windsor, D. (2001) "The future of corporate social responsibility", *The International Journal of Organizational Analysis,* Vol. 9, No. 3, pp. 225-256.

Wood, D. (1991) "Corporate social performance revisited", *Academy of Management Review,* Vol. 16, No. 4, pp. 691-718.

Wood, D. (2000- "Theory and integrity in business and society", *Business & Society,* Vol. 39, No. 4, pp. 359-378.

Environmental Obstacles and Support Factors of Social Entrepreneurship

Alina Badulescu, Sebastian Sipos-Gug and Adriana Borza

University of Oradea, Oradea, Romania

Abstract. Social entrepreneurship is a growing field of research, focused on generating businesses and activities related to social value creation and social missions. Even if it is a relatively new concept, its contribution in meeting effective needs not covered by the public sector justifies the increasing interest in approaching social entrepreneurship. As usual in emerging new research fields, studies have focused until recently on defining the concept and emphasizing the differences which distinguish social entrepreneurship from classical entrepreneurship. Relatively few studies have addressed the issue of the entrepreneurial process or factors influencing social entrepreneurship start–ups and their success. In this context, our paper aims to provide information and work towards a better understanding of the role played by environmental factors in this regard, as well as their perception among young people who intend to be or are involved in Romanian social enterprises. We used the methodological model proposed by the Global Entrepreneurship Monitor reports to identify individuals involved in social entrepreneurship, and we distinguished between hybrid social enterprises and entirely social non-governmental organizations. We further assessed the innovative dimension of these enterprises in order to identify change agents as opposed to classical NFP organizations. The social entrepreneurs identified with this method rated the impact of multiple environmental obstacles and support factors on achieving their social mission. The perception of these factors by the general population and students with social entrepreneurial intent was also assessed. A multinomial regression model was constructed, attempting to calculate the odds ratio of a person being either a social entrepreneur or intending to be one, compared to the general population, based only on the differences in environment hostility and munificence perception. A second hypothesis was that the perception of these environmental factors would be different amongst those who intend to start-up a social enterprise when compared to those who have already started. This was tested by using a t test, and subsequently the difference in perception, which we dubbed perception error, was introduced in our model. The main practical implication of this research was to bring to attention the need for a change in young individuals' perception of the threats and opportunities which they will face when starting and running a social enterprise. The perception errors inevitably affect their entrepreneurial intent and might prevent valuable individuals from entering the field. Social entrepreneurship trainings should therefore focus on fostering a realistic view of the environmental factors that might impact entrepreneurial success.

Keywords: social entrepreneurship, environmental obstacles, environmental munificence, entrepreneurial intent, perception error

1. Introduction

Due to new challenges that have arisen in the context of the global economic crisis of recent years, debates on entrepreneurship and its role in the contemporary life of communities acquires new meanings. A change in the focus of definitions of an entrepreneur in the literature reflects a certain tendency to see entrepreneurship as a vector of control of social relations rather than a purely economic approach.

It is considered that social entrepreneurship as a particular form of social and economic activity emerged only in the second half of the twentieth century. Certainly, early forms of social entrepreneurship existed in the past, generally associated with charitable activities. As Ghenea (2011, p. 61) stated, "perhaps the most remarkable example of social entrepreneurship in the classical period (nineteenth century in Victorian Britain) is Florence Nightingale, who developed the first school for nurses." It is generally accepted that this kind of business activity is not focused on immediate financial profit. Social entrepreneurship aims to be an effective approach, even if it follows the fulfillment of social objectives with broader community impact, rather than the personal profit of the entrepreneur. Maximizing money invested for the good of the community or for solving social problems remains a priority.

2. Conceptual framework

2.1. Specificity of social entrepreneurship

Social entrepreneurship has different objectives to those of a common enterprise, whose activities pursue financial performance by any means. It is "the entrepreneurial activity that starts from the identification of a social problem (e.g. in education, health, and on other social issues important to the community) and is based on solving the social problems through specifically entrepreneurial methods (by structuring an organization and finding solutions for action, funding and development of this organization)" (Ghenea 2011, p. 61). We can admit in these conditions that any form of social entrepreneurship is, in subsidiary, a form of political entrepreneurship. Social entrepreneurship is more strongly conditioned by a pre-existing framework of government policy and, in general, a particular ideological construct that exists in a society at a certain time. "When entrepreneurship desires new (forms of) sociality, the citizen's interest takes priority and new possibilities of life are the result. A shift from enterprising entrepreneurial Individuals to the relationships between citizens and fellow citizens " (Chell et al. 2010 in Hjorth 2013, p.6).

If we take Schumpeter's perspective on the entrepreneur (essentially as an innovative and ingenious individual and not as a manager of economic activities), then we have to admit that social entrepreneurship appears to be quite limited. It is clear from this perspective that when aiming at identifying and solving social problems, the social entrepreneur may seek only unconventional ways of solving widely known problems. The social entrepreneur's creativity has a fairly narrow range of expression, and radical solutions are only exceptions. If, as Schumpeter states, the entrepreneur is a person who "brings a dream to reality", social entrepreneurship is an extremely problematic demarche: the difficulties faced by a social entrepreneur are much larger than the resistance encountered in any typical entrepreneurial endeavor.

The social entrepreneur is not "a destroyer of the natural order" (in the words of Schumpeter's entrepreneurial classic). Perhaps on the contrary, he or she is a balancing agent who seeks to discover relationships that society at some point considers as abnormal. Deviation from the social norm is of course a contextual judgment. The social entrepreneur must clearly see the current of society in which he lives, but on the other hand he must be tough and strong enough to oppose this trend if he finds that the social effects of a given concept have a negative effects human life. Decisions must be taken by a social entrepreneur who is not working only on a classical analysis of cost-benefit. Precisely because of this, the social entrepreneur profile requires dimensions that classic entrepreneur profiles do not require.

Like any businessman, the social entrepreneur must be a speculator of opportunities. In his case, however, the major difference is related to the ethical framework which underpins every real opportunity. The classic entrepreneur will speculate on a market's weaknesses or regulatory vices with the sole purpose of profit. The social entrepreneur's decision always has a vigorous moral dimension, and both the public welfare and the good of the community represent a general purpose behind any activity of this type. It is assumed that the success of the social entrepreneur is strongly conditioned by a good resilience to failure, as to function effectively social entrepreneurship has to overcome a long series of public prejudices and mentality resistances. Albert Shapiro (1975) accounted between important features of entrepreneur and its ability to accept failures.

The fact that in many cases some non-profit organizations operate efficiently and provide services of social value does not automatically mean that their managers or administrators are social entrepreneurs. According to Peter and Waterman (1982) entrepreneurship is something beyond the solution of management discourse's diagnostic of what the Competitive Organization needs in a globalized economy. People who set up and manage small businesses or charitable organizations are usually not real entrepreneurs: they work to a template, and even if the initiative belongs to them, they merely carry out the same organization or business that already exists either in their area or somewhere outside the country where it operates. Sufficient examples of this exist, and they are not representative of social entrepreneurial activities in the area: we can regard these initiatives as extensions of entrepreneurial activity; social entrepreneurship, however, is characterized by the ability to stimulate and answer the new public requirements. Also the use of new management strategies is specific to social entrepreneurship.

In the case of social entrepreneurship, the managerial dimension of personality is well-defined: if "entrepreneurs rely too often on intuition and subjective beliefs" (Tanţău 2011, p.7), the social entrepreneur is forced to act on certain beliefs or concepts that have a common rational background. We do not refer to simple instrumental rationality, but a form of rationality which refers to moral and human principles and beliefs. We assume that social entrepreneurs make decisions and judge opportunities based on preliminary ideas of what constitutes freedom, public welfare, human rights and social progress. The interpretation of these differences is not unitary within the specialized research. The classic entrepreneur's desire to escape the constraints is interpreted by some authors as an additional form of responsibility. "Gabriele Euchner (2000) believes that entrepreneurs have stronger values than managers namely: Commitment means both responsibility and engagement..." (Tanţău 2011, p 7).

What appears less clear here is how the concept of responsibility is understood. The thinking of entrepreneurs and managers shares common ground, but there are a set of major differences. In the case of social entrepreneurs "desire for social change is then not over-coded by an interest in economic profit. While economic profit certainly is not excluded, it is balanced by seeking new sociality as result" (Hjorth 2013, p 35).

The entrepreneur is partisan to a flexibility that often exceeds the set of social values that animates the type of modern civilization that defends Christianity and generally publicly circulates in the Western world. Social entrepreneurship loses substance when it is disconnected from the values of modern civilization and our own culture. Social entrepreneurship targets ethical business and builds positive social impact; achieving this objective is only possible under constant connection to the world's values and modern European civilization.

2.2.   Social entrepreneurship in Romania

Given the widening debate on the theme of social , the increased interest in social entrepreneurship in all EU countries is only natural. In Romania, these debates are limited due to the lack of an adequate legal framework (the number of organizations engaged in social entrepreneurship is relatively small) especially in the context of economic crisis. As Dretcanu and Iorga (2012, p.7) stated, "in Romania there aren't so far clear and consistent regulations in the social economy, specific types of social economy organizations, operating principles, limitations or existing facilities....". There are also those who hold the opinion that in Romania there are still formulas that can be explained by "the silence of law". As Vîrjan (2011) states, the social economy in Romania is regulated, but not fostered and encouraged enough. "The existing legislative framework is governing some aspects of social economy entities, and those who want to practice social economy have to use legal artifices or seek other legal regulations as appropriate for that activity" (Vîrjan 2011, p.134).

The need for conceptual clarification is felt in the space of legal regulations of social entrepreneurship. The second round table organized at the initiative of the organization Act responsibly - CSR Social Network was held in January 2013 and focused on social entrepreneurship in Romania, and its opportunities and challenges. At the event, it was noted that "in the absence of a clear definition and measurement of social impact tools (audit performed by a third party) entities operating in the social economy sector, introducing incentives and non-financial measures of support may generate discrimination affecting competition in the free market or lead to abuses. In this regard, the need to improve the definition of the social economy, as it appears in social welfare law - in Law 292/2011 – was stressed" (CSR Media, 2013).

In the area of public policy in Romania, it is difficult to develop reliable measures as long as estimations regarding the consistently of social effects cannot be made. Either way, today social entrepreneurship appears at present as a support solution from inside EU community policies of sustainable development, and those aimed at generally creating a sustainable social environment. "A small but growing number of Europeans from central and eastern part, social reformers, were grouped as viable social enterprises and received support from international sources for their development. Although it has been considered as an alternative service for unemployment and human services, the concept of social enterprise in Central and Eastern Europe is starting already to reflect the realities recorded in the region "(Nicolaescu, 2011:80).

It is of course quite clear that in Romania, a country facing major economic problems, expansion of the culture of social entrepreneurship was not a government priority. However, in general society, amid increasingly intense action awareness, one can see an increased interest amongst entrepreneurs in sustainable development (Badulescu and Petria, 2013). "Rose-Ackerman (1996) argues that performance and survival rate of non-profit organizations and for profit depends not only on the institutional structure, but also the characteristics of business and entrepreneur motivation. It is obvious that nonprofit contractors must obtain a relatively high private result for having founded a nonprofit organization" (Nicolaescu, 2011:88).

The literature, consequently paints the picture of a hostile environment in Romania. Few studies, however, analyze the perception of this environment amongst present and future social entrepreneurs. Our research proposes to bring new evidence that this perception could influence the decision to start a social enterprise. Furthermore we argue that in this case the perception is more important than the objective factors. Young entrepreneurs might lose motivation if their perception of the environment is distorted towards adversity. These hypotheses are tested in the following section using empirical methods.

3. Research methodology

In the following sections we will describe the instruments and data analysis methodology.

3.1. Investigated variables

We will briefly present the instruments we used to gather data.

3.1.1. Social entrepreneurship

Social entrepreneurship was measured by using the methodology proposed by Lepoutre et al. (2013) for the GEM studies. We used the criteria they proposed to identify social entrepreneurs: first we evaluated the explicit social characteristics, then we selected only those enterprises that were self-sustaining, and then we evaluated innovation to differentiate between traditional NGOs and NFP social enterprises.

3.1.2. Environmental hostility and munificence

In order to evaluate the perception of environmental hostility and munificence, we compiled two scales specific for social entrepreneurship, starting from the existing instruments that study them in relation to general entrepreneurship (Baum and Wally 2003; Ruvio and Shoham 2011; Lin and Shih 2008; Scheepers et al. 2008). Primary analysis of scale characteristics yielded an internal consistency of 0.67 (omega total) for the environmental munificence scale, and 0.79 (omega total) for the environmental hostility scale. These omega values are considered to be adequate, albeit a bit small.

3.1.3. Influence and strength of external factors

We also gathered information regarding the participants' perception of the impact of various external factors (i.e. Competitors, Government, Law, Labour market, Economy, Ecology, Demographics, External Politics and European Union) on the enterprises ability to achieve their goals This measure differs from that of environmental hostility and munificence in that we are interested in the direction of these effects (positive or negative), but also on their perceived strength. This reflects the amount of control entrepreneurs feel they have over their enterprise, compared to external influences. Initial scale analysis yielded an internal consistency of 0.9 (omega total). This value is generally considered to be high, therefore suggesting strong internal consistency.

3.1.4. Social entrepreneurship intent

Social entrepreneurial intent was evaluated using a multiple response intent scale. The scale's possible answers were "No intent now, or in the future", "I intend to do so in the next two years, but I don't have a specific plan", "I intend to do so in the next two years, and I have already started preparing for it" and "I am currently volunteering in a social enterprise". We did not force a single answer, but no participant choose more than one option. We then divided the participants based on their answers in for groups. We labelled them "no intent", "general intent", "specific intent" and "volunteering", respectively.

3.2. Data gathering

Data was gathered in February – March 2013, using an online form that was distributed to both enterprises and students acting in social enterprises in Romania. We invited 517 enterprises to participate in the study, and after applying the selection criteria of self-sustainability, we identified 28 social enterprises, according to the broad definition (social goal), and 23 social enterprises, according to the narrow definition (social goal and social innovation). We choose to use the 28 enterprises selected according to the self-sustainability criterion, as it allows for more statistical power in our analysis.

We also invited 210 students to participate, and after initial validation 208 were used in the study. 2 were removed due to a high number of missing values. Their distribution according to the entrepreneurial intent scale is shown in Figure 1. All participants volunteered for the study, and their answers were anonymous and confidential.

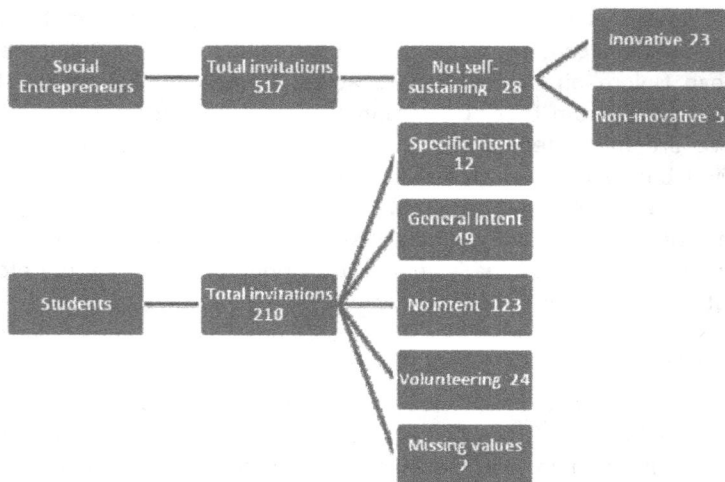

Figure 1: Participant selection flow-chart (only one 'n' in innovative)

3.3. Data analysis

Data analysis was conducted using PASW Statistics 18.0. Missing value analysis was conducted, and after removing 2 students with more than 6 missing values, the rest of the cases showed no pattern of missing data. There were a total of 8 missing values in the dataset (0.04% of total data), and in the interest of preserving the rest of the data they were included in the analysis where possible.

4. Results

4.1. Descriptive data analysis

As shown in Table 1 and Figure 2, all the factors are perceived to have a positive impact on the performance of social enterprises, with the exception of the Economy in general as perceived by social entrepreneurs. There are some differences, most notably between entrepreneurs and the general intent category. We shall investigate these differences in detail in section 4.3.

118

Table 1: Perception of environmental factors influence on social enterprise performance

Factor	Entrepreneurs	No intent	General intent
Competition with NGOs	38.00	34.7619	46.80851
Competition with FPOs	6.00	19.36937	30.61224
Government	16.00	8.849558	7.446809
Law	12.96	13.47826	13.54167
Labour Market	20.37	29.09091	35.41667
Economy	-14.29	20.72072	19.38776
Ecology	16.67	20.58824	21.73913
Demographics	33.33	39.44954	29.34783
External policy	22.00	20.29703	27.90698
European Union	40.38	50.92593	39.13043

Figure 2 also allows us to see a general pattern. Entrepreneurs seem to constantly evaluate the environmental factors as less positive then the other categories. This offers initial support for our main hypothesis, that a perception bias exists, and that this bias, or error, might influence even the decision to become a social entrepreneur.

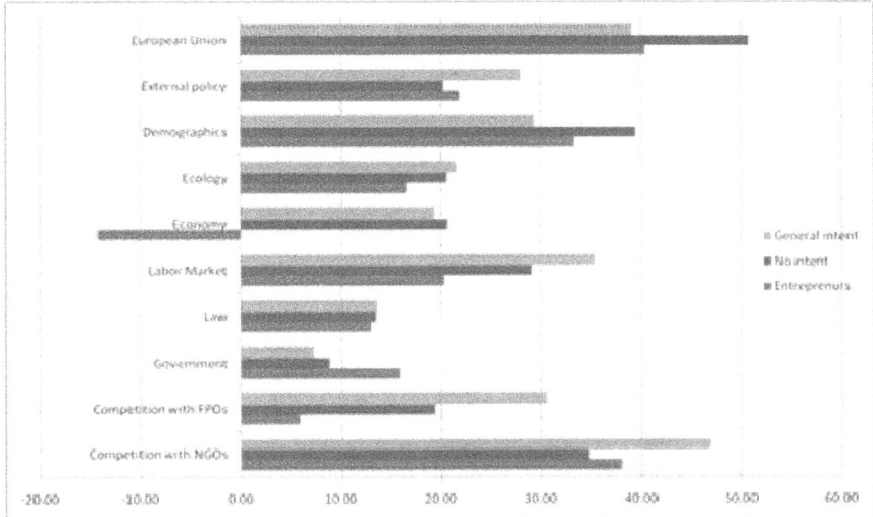

Figure 2: Graphical comparison of the perception of environmental factors' influence on social enterprise performance among groups

4.2. A predictive model of social entrepreneurial intent

The first hypothesis we tested was that a model could be constructed by which we can predict social entrepreneurial intent based on the perception of environmental factors. For this purpose, since we are conducting a prospective study, we decided to use a multinomial logistic regression model, as it has low requirements regarding data structure and distributions.

The levels used in the dependent variable were specific intent, intent, volunteering activity and no intent. The reference category used was no intent.

Table 2 shows the model fitting information. As can be observed, the model's likelihood ratio test has an associated p value lower then 0.05, thus suggesting that at least one of the variables inserted into the model could be a significant predictor.

Table 2: Model fitting information

Model	AIC	-2 Log Likelihood	Chi-Square	df	Sig.
Intercept Only	447.649	441.649			
Final	441.839	417.839	23.811	9	.005

Table 3 shows that all three variables introduced into the model have parameters significantly different from 0, and therefore eliminating them from the model would not improve it. This can also be observed by comparing AIC values of the reduced models, as they are all higher than the full model value.

Table 4 shows the parameter estimates of the proposed model. As one can see from this table, the odds ratio of the specific intent group does not seem to be influenced significantly by any of the investigated variables.

However in the case of the general intent group the odds ratio are significantly influenced by perceived environmental hostility, munificence and the perceived strength of external influence. More specifically perceiving the environment as being more hostile decreases the odds of an individual to be in the entrepreneurial intent group by 1.618 times. Perceiving the environment as being more munificent increases those odds by 1.611 times, while perceiving the external influences as being stronger further increases those odds by 1.161 times.

Table 3: Model likelihood ratio tests

Effect	Model Fitting Criteria		Likelihood Ratio Tests		
	AIC of Reduced Model	-2 Log Likelihood of Reduced Model	Chi-Square	df	Sig.
Intercept	442.099	424.099	6.260	3	.100
Environmental hostility	447.606	429.606	11.767	3	.008
Environmental munificence	445.628	427.628	9.790	3	.020
Strength of external factors	444.965	426.965	9.126	3	.028

In the case of the Volunteering group, the only significant influence seems to be exerted by the Perception of Environmental Hostility. Namely, perceiving the environment as being more hostile decreases the odds of someone being in this group by 1.964 times.

4.3. Measuring the perception bias

A second hypothesis of our study was that the perception of environmental factors differs significantly between those with social entrepreneurial intent and those who are active social entrepreneurs.

We started by testing for general assumptions of normality and equality of variances. For normality we used the Kolmogorov-Smirnoff test, which yielded in all cases p values higher than 0.05, therefore we have failed to reject the hypothesis that the distributions are different from the normal distribution. For testing the equality of variances we used the Levene test, which also yielded in all cases p values higher than 0.05, therefore we cannot reject the hypothesis that the distributions have equal variances.

Table 4: Parameter estimates of the proposed model (needs realignment)

		B	Std. Error	Wald	df	Sig.	Exp(B)
Specific intent	Intercept	-2.381	1.679	2.012	1	.156	
	Environmental hostility	.157	.342	.210	1	.647	1.170
	Environmental munificence	-.264	.328	.647	1	.421	.768
	Strength of external factors	.068	.086	.621	1	.431	1.070
General Intent	Intercept	-2.339	1.091	4.599	1	.032	
	Environmental hostility	-.481	.200	5.795	1	.016	.618
	Environmental munificence	.477	.186	6.547	1	.011	1.611
	Strength of external factors	.150	.052	8.175	1	.004	1.161
Volunteering	Intercept	-1.248	1.287	.940	1	.332	
	Environmental hostility	-.676	.257	6.943	1	.008	.509
	Environmental munificence	.396	.232	2.922	1	.087	1.486
	Strength of external factors	.087	.065	1.777	1	.182	1.091

The pseudo R squared value for our model was 0.123 using the Nagelkerke method, therefore the proportion of the total variability that is accounted by the model is 12.3%.

Having met the requirements for using the independent samples t test, we proceeded by comparing the social entrepreneurs group with the social entrepreneurial intent group. The results are presented in Table 5 for the specific intent group and Table 6 for the general intent group.

Table 5: Levene and t tests for the comparison of social entrepreneurs group and the specific intent group

Scale	Levene		T test		
	F	Sig.	t	df	Sig. (2-tailed)
Environmental hostility	0.260	0.613	0.621	38.000	0.539
Environmental munificence	1.910	0.175	0.987	38.000	0.330
Strength of external factors	0.778	0.383	-1.222	38.000	0.229

In the case of the students with specific social entrepreneurial intent all the t tests have associated p values higher then 0.05, therefore we cannot claim that the differences between the two groups are statistically significant.

Table 6: Levene and t test for the comparison of social entrepreneurs group and the general intent group

Scale	Levene		T test		
	F	Sig.	t	df	Sig. (2-tailed)
Environmental hostility	1.287	.260	1.992	75	.050
Environmental munificence	1.464	.230	-.007	75	.994
Strength of external factors	.002	.961	-2.714	75	.008

In the case of the general social entrepreneurial intent group the results are shown in Table 6. For the Environmental munificence the t test has an associated p value higher then 0.05, therefore we cannot claim that the differences between the two groups are statistically significant. In the case of Environmental hostility and the perceived Strength of external factors there exists a statistically significant difference between the two groups (p = 0.05, and p = 0.008 respectively).

We can conclude that the general entrepreneurial intent group has a lower perception of Environmental hostility then the social entrepreneurs group

(m_1 = 4.34 and m_2 = 4.95, respectively), and a higher perception of the Strength of external factors (m_1 = 9.39 and m_2 = 7.36, respectively).

4.4. Correcting for perception bias

For the interest of our study we assume that the social entrepreneurs already operating on the market have an accurate perception of environmental factors, and therefore any significant difference from them would be due to the perception error of those unfamiliar with the field.

In order to assess the influence the perception bias might play on social entrepreneurial intent we decided to compare the predictive model constructed earlier with a second model, which would include a corrected perception bias. For our purpose the correction used was the average difference between groups. This serves to move the average, while not artificially changing the variance due to random error.

The corrected values were introduced into a second predictive model.

As shown in Table 7, this model no longer offers superior predictive capabilities when compared with simply using the average. This is also evidenced by a decrease in AIC of the model when variables are removed from the model.

Table 7: Model Fitting Information of the Perception Bias Corrected Model

Model	AIC	-2 Log Likelihood	Chi-Square	df	Sig.
Intercept Only	449.036	443.036			
Final	453.102	429.102	13.933	9	.125

Removing the perception error from the investigated variables no longer allows for a valid multinomial logistic model, therefore no other statistical analyses could be performed.

5. Conclusions

Our study successfully built a predictive model of social entrepreneurial intent of students, based on their perception of Environmental hostility, munificence and the strength of external factors. While the model cannot distinguish between those with strong intent (who have already started their business plan) and those with no intent, thus suggesting that their perceptions might be similar, it is successful in identifying those with general intent (want to start a social enterprise in the next two years, but haven't started working on specific business plan) and those who do volunteer work for social enterprises.

Perceiving the environment as more munificent, less hostile and with stronger external factors significantly increase the odds of a student being in the general intent group, as opposed to the no intent group. Perceiving the environment as less hostile, alone, seems to increase the odds of someone being in the volunteering group as compared to the no intention group. The main limit of the model used is that it doesn't allow for causal inferences, and it serves mainly for exploratory purposes. However we decided to conduct further analyses in order to better understand this relationship.

We found that there exists a significant difference in perception between the general intent group and working social entrepreneurs, and we decided to see how correcting for this perception error might affect our predictive model. However after performing the corrections, no model could be constructed that predicts data better than the group averages. While this is not causal evidence for the influence of perception error on social entrepreneurial intent, it is indirect evidence that such a causal relationship might exist, as correcting for perception error reduced the models capability to accurately predict categories. Based on our results we recommend that this relationship be investigated further, as it might provide an explanation for the low success rate of new social enterprises. A more positive perception of the environmental factors that influence the workings of a social enterprise might attract more students to the field, however if this perception if not accurate it might lead to early abandonment of businesses. Further studies will need to clarify this relationship, and perhaps lead to a causal model.

References

Badulescu, D. and Petria, N. (2013), "Social Responsibility of Romanian Companies: Contribution to a "Good Society" or Expected Business Strategy?", *9th International Conference on "European Integration - New Challenges" – EINCO*, 24-25 May 2013, University of Oradea, Faculty of Economic Sciences

Baum, J.R. and Wally, S. (2003) "Strategic decision speed and firm performance", *Strategic Management Journal*, 24(11), pp1107–1129.

Dretcanu M. D. and Iorga E. (2012) Institute for Social Economy: the third sector. Recommendations for the proper functioning of social enterprises in Romania, Bucureşti [online] www.ipp.ro/protfiles.php?IDfile=168.

Ghenea, Marius (2011) *Entrepreneurship. The road from idea to business opportunities and business ideas*, Bucharest, Legal Universe Publishing.

Hjorth, Daniel (2013) "Public entrepreneurship: desiring social change, creating sociality", *Entrepreneurship and Regional Development*, Vol. 25, No. 1–2, January 2013, pp 34–51.

Lepoutre, J. et al. (2013) "Designing a global standardized methodology for measuring social entrepreneurship activity: The Global Entrepreneurship Monitor social entrepreneurship study". *Small Business Economics*, 40, pp 693–714.

Lin, H.-C. and Shih, C.-T. (2008) "How Executive SHRM System Links to Firm Performance: The Perspectives of Upper Echelon and Competitive Dynamics". *Journal of Management*, 34(5), pp 853–881.

McMullen, J. S. (2011) Delineating the domain of development entrepreneurship: A market-based Approach to facilitating inclusive economic growth. Entrepreneurship Theory and Practice, 35 (1), pp 185-193.

Nicolăescu, Victor (2011) "Social enterprise in the contemporary socioeconomic context", *Social Economic Journal,* No. 1.

Ruvio, A. and Shoham, A. (2011) "A multilevel study of nascent social ventures". *International Small Business Journal*, 29(5), pp 562–579.

Peters, T. and Waterman, R. (1982) "In Search of Excellence". Newark: Harper and Row Publishers.

Scheepers, M., Hough, J. and Bloom, J. (2008) The development of an instrument to assess the enacted environment for corporate entrepreneurship in South Africa. *Management Dynamics*, 17(4), pp 2–18.

Tanţău A. Dumitru (2011) *Entrepreneurship. Innovative thinking and pragmatic*, Ed. C. H. Beck, Bucuresti.

Vîrjan, Daniela (2011) "Social economy and the labor market in the current context", *Journal of Social Economics*, No. 1, p 134 [online] http://profitpentruoameni.ro/wp-content/uploads/2012/03/Revista-de-Economie-Sociala-Nr.-1_2011.pdf

Alina Badulescu, Sebastian Sipos-Gug and Adriana Borza

*** http://www.csrmedia.ro/masa-rotunda-antreprenoriatul-social-in-romania-oportunitati-si-provocari/ accesed 20.03.2013

Portuguese Social Stock Exchange – Assessment of Sustainability

Teresa Costa and Luísa Carvalho

Economics and Management Department, Business School, Setúbal Polytechnic Institute, Portugal

Abstract: Social organizations have an important role detecting and exploring social opportunities. Frequently they are the solution to social problems where market and government fail. The social entrepreneurs identify and solve social problems where the others just see barriers, identifying and evaluating opportunities, disseminating new approaches and proposing sustainable solutions that contribute to the creation of social value. This article first presents a literature review about social entrepreneurship, social innovation and social entrepreneurs, considering different approaches and perspectives. Secondly, through a qualitative methodology, it studies the projects included in Social Stock Exchange (BVS). BVS replicates the atmosphere of a stock exchange and its role is to approach civil society organizations and social investors that are available to support these organizations by purchasing their social shares. This project is developing innovative approaches to attract financial resources in order to solve social problems, including the eradication of poverty and other social risks. Through the promotion of social investment, the BVS proposes an innovative financial model supported not in a philanthropy or charity perspective, but deciding according to the social profit of each project. The empirical study based on interviews applied to key-informers from social projects included in BVS. The interviews have three main objectives: 1- Identify the degree of project attractiveness; 2-Understand the reasons of project attractiveness in terms of funding; 3-Assess the sustainability of the projects, in an economic dimension (eg. job creation), social dimension (eg. resolution of a social need for a vulnerable group) and environmental dimension (eg. reduction of impacts on the environment). We believe that this paper contributes to a better understanding of the factors that promote the attractiveness of social projects and highlight the importance of improvement concerning management practices.

Keywords: case study, social entrepreneurship, social stock exchange, social value, sustainability

1. A framework of social entrepreneurship

The conceptualization of social entrepreneurship, similarly to the definition of entrepreneurship, has not met with consensus. This is an area of knowledge that is still young, and this is reflected in the variety of definitions in the literature (Seelos and Mair 2005). Another peculiarity of this approach relates to the possibility of social entrepreneurship emerging in various contexts; however, most studies refers to the public domain (Lewis, 1980; King and Roberts, 1987). As Venkataraman (1997, p. 120) notes, "there are fundamentally different conceptions and interpretations of the concept of entrepreneur and the entrepreneurial role, consensus on a definition of the field in terms of the entrepreneur is perhaps an impossibility." In this context we can identify different approaches in the literature on social entrepreneurship.

To better understand social entrepreneurship, Austin et al. (2006) differentiate two types of entrepreneurship. For these authors, commercial entrepreneurship represents the identification, evaluation, and exploitation of opportunities that result in profits. In contrast, social entrepreneurship refers to the identification, evaluation, and exploitation of opportunities that result in social value. Social entrepreneurs have a sensitive understanding of social needs, and answer to these needs through creative solutions. This attention to social value is present in various definitions of social entrepreneurship (e.g., Peredo and McLean, 2006; Shaw and Carter, 2007). The main difference between these two definitions of entrepreneurship (commercial and social) is the focus on social value versus private value.

Other perspectives can be found in the literature. According to Dees (1998a), social entrepreneurship refers to new non-profit ventures, as well as business ventures for social purposes, including community development banks and for-profit hybrid organizations. Austin et al. (2006, p. 2) define social entrepreneurship as an "innovative, social value creating activity that can occur within or across the nonprofit, business, or government sectors". These authors consider three primary ways to distinguish between commercial and social entrepreneurship.

Firstly, new commercial and social ventures diverge in terms of overall mission. While commercial entrepreneurs are primarily concerned with private gain, social entrepreneurs are more interested in creating social value. Nevertheless, commercial entrepreneurs may also produce social value in the process of creating private gain, and on the other hand, social entrepreneurs may produce private gain in the process of creating social value (Emerson and Twersky, 1996). However, with the exception of secondary gain, these two types of organizations are guided by two very different missions.

Secondly, commercial and social entrepreneurship differ severely in terms of performance measurement (Austin et al., 2006). For the first type performance is measured in terms of financial performance (i.e. profitability, sales growth); for the second type performance measures are less standardized and more particular to certain organizations (the measure can vary by the type of organization, i.e., educational or other). However, an effort has been made to minimize this difficulty, through the development of mechanisms that can help to alleviate this subject and the creation of new metrics to quantify value in the social sector (Young, 2006). The performance metrics, such as sales, profits or other traditional financial measures are mostly more suitable to commercial entrepreneurship. Social entrepreneurship includes more esoteric measures, such as lives touched, trees saved or percent of emissions reduced. However it is important that social entrepreneurs measure their impact on society or the environment. Most social projects must identify their own non-financial metrics of success based on their mission, industry, and ideal impact. Clearly, the metrics measured need to be positively correlated with the traditional financial measures, or the venture will not sustain over time.

Thirdly, commercial and social entrepreneurship diverge in terms of resource mobilization (Austin et al., 2006). Regarding the ability to obtain financial resources, business entrepreneurs have an advantage over social entrepreneurs: the perspective of potential profits. That is the motivation of business angels and venture capitalists. Another advantage relates to human resources: commercial entrepreneurs are able to hire employees based on the same factor, potential returns. When individuals decide to work for commercial entrepreneurs, they expect financial rewards in return for their performance, such as wages, benefits, future windfalls (i.e. stock options), or others.

Costa and Carvalho, 2011, tried to group the various definitions of social entrepreneurship, having identified three major groups:

- First group: social entrepreneurship refers to the initiatives of social organizations in search of alternative financing strategies or as a way of creating social value through management practices (Dees, 1998a; Austin, Stevenson and Wei-Skiller, 2006; Boschee, 1998).

- Second group: social entrepreneurship concerns the independent initiatives for social entrepreneurs who seek to alleviate a social problem and catalyze social transformation (Alvord, 2002; Alvord, 2004).

- Third group: social entrepreneurship includes a set of practices of social responsibility of companies involved in partnerships with other sectors (Sagawa and Segal, 2000; Waddock, 1988).

In conclusion, and despite the differences between social and commercial entrepreneurship, organizations can pursue commercial entrepreneurship, social entrepreneurship, or some combination of both (Austin et al., 2006; Peredo and McLean, 2006). In fact, some scholars advocate that organizations can have both commercial and social objectives, can work as *hybrids* (Davis, 1997), and in this case have two bottom lines, one related to profits and other related to social value.

2. Social entrepreneurship and social innovation

Phills Jr., Deiglmeier and Miller (2008) expand the field of investigation from social entrepreneurship to "social innovation". According to these authors social innovation is a novel answer to a social problem that is more effective, efficient and sustainable than the existing solutions, that creates value added to society as a whole rather than to private individuals. This first approach creates a great differentiation between private problems and social problems, as well as between private value and social value. This restricted view of social innovation has evolved. The evolution was made through the definition of social value by these authors; they defined social value as the creation of benefits or reductions of costs for society, trying to meet social needs and problems in a way that goes far beyond the private gains and general benefits of market activity.

According with Leadbeater (2007, p:2), "All innovation involves the application of new ideas – or the reapplication of old ideas in new ways – to devise better solutions to our needs. Innovation is invariably a cumulative, collaborative activity in which ideas are shared, tested, refined, developed and applied. Social innovation applies this thinking to social issues: education and health, issues of inequality and inclusion."

For Mulgan et al. (2007), social innovation refers to innovative activities and services that are moved by the goal of meeting a social need and that are mainly developed and diffused through organisations whose primary purposes are social. This definition differentiates social innovation from business innovations. The last are usually focused on profit maximisation and diffused through organisations that mainly moved by profit maximisation. However we can find some borderline cases, such as models of distance learning that first appeared in social organisations but then were adopted by businesses. For these authors the most interesting innovations are those that take the form of replicable programmes or organisations, referring the spread of cognitive behavioural therapy of Aaron Beck in the 1960s, then tested empirically in the 1970s and later extend to professional and policy networks as a good examples of social innovation,. The Social Stock Exchange can also be regarded as an example of social innovation. In this case, a replication of the atmosphere of a stock exchange has been made. This environment creates a network that facilitates the relationships between Civil Society Organizations that create social value in the area of education and entrepreneurship, and social investors (donors) that support these organizations by purchasing their social actions.

3. Sources of opportunities and resources cooptation

The recognition and exploitation of opportunities is a key issue in social entrepreneurship (Austin et al., 2006; Mair and Marti, 2006): it is worth considering that social entrepreneurship has particular features, distinct from the usual commercial opportunities (Austin et al., 2006; Dorado, 2006; Mair, 2006; Robinson, 2006). Several authors point out the uniqueness of social opportunities in comparison with commercial opportunities:

- Social entrepreneurship opportunities are focused on social problems and they involve attempts to create social value (Dees, 2001; Thompson, 2002). Social value creation concerns the resolution of social issues, in such actions as generating income for the economically disadvantaged or delivering medical supplies to poverty-stricken areas of the globe, and requires innovation just as economic value creation does in the commercial sector (Dees, 2001, 2007). Opportunities to create social value surface through philanthropic activities, social activism, such as fair trade importing, and through notions of self-help that engender systems enabling people to help themselves similar to the microfinance movement (Hockerts, 2006).

- Social entrepreneurship opportunities can be distinct according the context where these opportunities surface and could be recognized, and exploited.

Indeed, social problems (people) and environmental problems (planet) are presented as opportunities for social entrepreneurs (Neck et al, 2009). The identification and exploitation of opportunities provides solutions to social problems, such as a lack of healthcare or education, poverty and hunger, and new technologies and innovations to solve such environmental problems as energy shortages, water shortages, and global warming.

Entrepreneurial projects require resources and, just as traditional entrepreneurs, social entrepreneurs must find a range of tools and strategies to attract the resources. Entrepreneurship literature (Aldrich and Zimmer, 1986; Birley, 1985; Johannisson, 2000) provides several studies on entrepreneurial networks and their fundamental role in providing access to knowledge, information, and resources. Some of those studies highlight strategies followed by entrepreneurs in order to attract resources, such as, the use of networks and social resourcing, financial bootstrapping, strategies of effectuation (Domenico et al, 2010).

Some studies in field of social entrepreneurship exemplify cases of the resources acquisition through networks that are tangible (in the case of capital and physical assets) and others that are relational. It is possible to note that entrepreneurs frequently use such personal networks as kinship ties and family mentors in order to access support, skills, and experience, thereby facilitating market penetration (Domenico et al, 2010).

4. Methodology

This empirical research applies the case study methodology. According to Yin (1994) a case study method is most suitable for an investigation that asks such questions as "how" and "why", over which the researcher has little or no control. Yin (1994) defines the case study research method as an empirical study that investigates a contemporary phenomenon within its real-life context; when the limits between phenomenon and context are not clearly evident; and in which multiple sources of evidence are used (Yin, 1994, p. 13). This exploratory study adopted an iterative process of data collection in conducting a case study built on the results of a semi-structured interviews (see Annex 1 – Interview guide) applied to key-informers involved with projects included in BVS. The interviews were conducted during March and April 2012. The study also used documental sources of information available in BVS and projects websites and other documents.

5. Empirical study

5.1. Portuguese social stock exchange - BVS

The BVS includes several projects in various areas, with results in education and social entrepreneurship. Through the analysis of the projects it was possible to find solutions to social needs in different contexts, mostly in disadvantaged or excluded social groups. The model of funding proposed by BVS allows the attraction of financial resources with transparency and creativity. This social stock market re-creates the social environment of a stock exchange involving the civil organizations and social investors. Thus is it possible to promote social investment, challenging the social investor not to participate from the perspective of philanthropy and charity, but from the choice of which investment might generate social profit.

5.2. Analysis of BVS projects

The data analyses of information collected allowed the achievement of the main objectives of the study. The interpretation of the information is organized according to the three objectives listed. Table 1 organizes the information related to the degree of project attractiveness, Table 2 structures the reasons for project attractiveness in terms of funding and, finally, Table 3 presents a sustainability assessment of the projects. In order to identify the degree of project attractiveness, Table 1 identifies the projects currently available in BVS, in April 2012, presenting the project value, shares sold and the percentage of funding generated.

Table 1: Value and funding of BVS projects (data results) (caught across page)

Project name	Project value	Shares sold	% Funding
"Centro ABCReal Portugal"	50.000,00	160,00	0,32%
"Polo Social Manto"	42.872,00	20.677,00	48,23%
"Projeto Viver, Crescer e Integrar"	22.100,00	2.034	9,20%
"Social Innovation Challenge"	15.200,00	5.549,00	36,51%
"A Vida Vale"	50.000,00	10.469,00	20,94%
"Agência ODM"	160.000,00	71.100,00	44,44%
"Audiodescrição.pt – ouço, logo vejo"	20.000,00	20.000,00	100,00%
"Capital Aldeia"	94.500,00	1.295,00	1,37%
"Casa da Cidadania"	150.000,00	1.490,00	0,99%
"Centro de Interpretação da Abelha"	229.765,00	43.445,00	18,91%
"Cidadania Plena"	72.720,00	571,00	0,79%
"Cozinhar o Futuro"	165.000,00	165.000,00	100,00%
"Crescer Com Afetividade"	68.500,00	650,00	0,95%
"Crescer dos 8 aos 80"	80.648,00	21.556,00	26,73%
"EC3, Eco-Centro de Compostagem Caseira"	38.644,00	135,00	0,35%
"Educação é a Melhor Prevenção"	200.000,00	2.885,00	1,44%
"EfeitoD"	97.388,00	48.128,00	49,42%
"Formar Campões para a Vida"	53.880,00	1.240,00	2,30%
"Lar Telhadinho"	200.000,00	4.441,00	2,22%

Project name	Project value	Shares sold	% Funding
"Lavandaria Solidária"	164.733,00	46.935,00	28,49%
"Mais Cuidados, Mais Integrados"	20.470,00	15,00	0,07%
"Passos de Tempo"	46.420,00	12.364,00	26,64%
"Piscina Terapêutica os 4 Elementos"	118.000,00	1.856,00	1,57%
"Por ti" – Projecto de Apoio a ti	14.835,00	2.636,00	17,77%
"Porto de Abrigo"	129.600	2.855	2,20%
"Retalhos de Esperança"	5.000,00	5.000,00	100,00%
"Rir é o melhor remédio?"	134.000,00	28.988,00	21,63%
"Saúde a Sorrir"	112.376,00	2.148,00	1,91%
"Semear o Futuro"	100.000,00	27.012,00	27,01%
"Serviço de Intervenção e Apoio à Criança"	58.469,00	4.633,00	7,92%
"UMAD"	50.000,00	50.000,00	100,00%

Source: The Authors

It can be seen that 48% of the projects have less than 10% funding (15 projects), 7% (2 projects) have funding higher than 10% and lower than 20%, 19% (6 projects) have funding higher than 20% and lower than 30%, 3% (1 project) have funding higher than 30% and lower than 40%, 10/ (3 projects) have funding higher than 40% and lower than 50% and finally 13% of the projects (4 projects) have 100% funding.

This analysis suggests that the attractiveness of the projects can vary, and their funding may depends on several factors, such as the social entrepreneurs' pro-activity, the stakeholders' involvement, the age of the project, the region and the type of public target.

In order to understand the reasons of this attractiveness, certain features of the projects were studied: initial date, region, scope of activities, type of organization (Social Solidarity Institutions – public or private), entrepreneur pro-activity, stakeholders' participation and public target (see Table 2).

Analysis of Table 2 does not reveal a similar pattern between the projects in BVS and their funding. Nevertheless, the analysis of the projects with full funding allows for the identification of some common vectors. The four projects with 100% funding are:

- "Cozinhar o Futuro":an innovative project that aims to prepare the future for young mothers - mostly single mothers belonging to disadvantaged social classes. The project provides professional training and support teenage mothers with a sustainable living project.

- "UMAD": a van equipped with a doctor's office and medical staff. The project provides home health care to children, keeping them in their homes, and simultaneously helping families to gain autonomy in the processes associated with their treatment.

- "Audiodescrição.pt": this project aims the implementation of audio description in all artistic and cultural events in the country. This technological resource allows understanding of scenarios and environments, facial expressions, body language, input and output of characters from the scene, as well as other types of action, used in television, film, theatre, museums, exhibitions and other art forms, to complement artistic and cultural expression for the blind.

- "Retalhos de Esperança": through this project unemployed women from Madeira Island recycle donated clothing and produce new home clothes.

Project name	Public target	% Funding	Date	Scope activity	NUT II	Geographic scope	Public Institution
"Centro ABC Real Portugal"	Autistic children and young people	0,32%	2011	Education/Special Education	Lisbon	National	Yes
"Polo Social Manto"	Disadvantaged communities	48,23%	2011	Social entrepreneurship /Socio-Economic development	Lisbon	National	Yes
"Projeto Viver, Crescer e Integrar"	Immigrant population	9,20%	2011	Education for citizenship	Lisbon	National	No
"Social Innovation Challenge"	Students (high school)	36,51%	2011	Education/ education for sustainability	Lisbon	National	Yes
"A Vida Vale"	The edery	20,94%	2011	Entrepreneurship/Socio-Economic development	Alentejo	Regional	Yes
"Agência ODM"	Students in higher education	44,44%	2009	Education for citizenship	Lisbon	National	Yes
"Audiodescrição.pto"	People with visual disabilities	100,00%	2010	Education/ education for sustainability	Lisbon	Regional	No
"Capital Aldeia"	Rural population of the village of Safara	1,37%	2009	Social entrepreneurship /Socio-Economic development	Alentejo	Regional	No
"Casa da Cidadania"	Different social groups	0,99%	2010	Education for citizenship	Algarve	Regional	Yes
"Centro de Interpretação da Abelra"	Beekeepers in the village of Terra Chã	18,91%	2009	Social entrepreneurship /Socio-Economic development	Centro	Regional	No
"Cidadania Plena"	Women immigrants - brazil and African countries (portuguese language)	0,79%	2010	Education for citizenship	Lisbon	Regional	No

Project name	Public target	% Funding	Date	Scope activity	NUT II	Geographic scope	Public Institution
"Cozinhar o Futuro"	Teenage mothers	100,00%	2010	Social entrepreneurship / Funding	Lisbon	Regional	Yes
"Crescer Com Afetividade"	Marginalized youth	0,95%	2011	Social entrepreneurship	Norte	Regional	No
"Crescer dos 8 aos 80"	Families from disadvantaged classes	26,73%	2010	Education for citizenship	Lisbon	Regional	Yes
"EC3. Eco-Centro de Compostagem Caseira"	Children from kindergarten to secondary level	0,35%	2011	Education/ education for sustainability	Alentejo	Regional	No
"Educação é a Melhor Prevenção"	Children, parents and grandparents	1,44%		Education/ education for sustainability	Centro	Internacional	Yes
"FeitoD"	Patients with trisomy 21	49,42%	2009	Social entrepreneurship	Lisbon	National	Yes
"Formar Campeões para a Vida"	Children and youth at risk	2,30%	2011	Education for citizenship	Lisbon	National	No
"Lar Telhadinho"	People with disabilities and their families	2,22%	2010	Social entrepreneurship /Socio-Economic development	Lisbon	Regional	Yes
"Lavandaria Solidária"	Vulnerable social groups	28,49%	2011	Social Entrepreneurship / Job creation	Centro	Regional	Yes
"Mais Cuidados, Mais Integrados"	Ethnic minorities	0,07%	2011	Social entrepreneurship /Socio-Economic development	Centro	Regional	Yes
"Passos de Tempo"	The elderly	26,64%	2010	Education for citizenship	Lisbon	Regional	No
"Piscina Terapêutica os 4 Elementos"	People with disabilities	1,57%	2010	Education / Special Education	Centro	Regional	Yes

Project name	Public target	% Funding	Date	Scope activity	NUT II	Geographic scope	Public Institution
"Porti" – Projecto de Apoio a ti	Families with low incomes	17,77%	2010	Education for citizenship	Lisbon	Regional	Yes
"Porto de Abrigo"	Disadvantaged youths and adults, from 16 years old, with intellectual development problems	2,20%	2010	Social entrepreneurship	Lisbon	National	Yes
"Retalhos de Esperança"	Unemployed women	100,10%	2011	Social entrepreneurship /Socio-Economic development	Madeira Region	Regional	Yes
"Rir é o melhor remédio?"	Hospitalized children, families, health professionals	21,63%	2009	Entrepreneurship	Lisbon	Regional	Yes
"Saúde a Sorrir"	Disadvantaged, excluded or marginalized communities	1,91%	2010	Social entrepreneurship	Norte	Regional	Yes
"Semear o Futuro"	People with hearing impairments and autism	27,01%	2010	Social entrepreneurship / Funding	Lisbon	Regional	Yes
"Serviço de Intervenção e Apoio à Criança"	Children with disabilities	7,92%	2010	Special Education	Lisbon	Regional	Yes

The first two projects are projects with a high involvement of different stakeholders and sponsors. The third project also has the important involvement of various stakeholders. They are linked with reputable organizations which have a wide contact network and a history of successful projects, suggesting some variables, such as historical and organization seniority, entrepreneur pro-activity, stakeholders participation.

The fourth project has a more regional scope and is on a smaller scale in terms of funding and public targets, suggesting that local participation is crucial for the success of this kind of project, in which the community is the main partner.

This analysis concerning the reasons for projects' attractiveness suggest similar tendencies to other studies cited in the literature review. These reveal the importance of the strategies followed by entrepreneurs in order to attract resources, such as, the use of networks and social resourcing, financial bootstrapping, strategies of effectuation (Domenico et al, 2010).

Finally, the sustainability of these projects was assessed, taking into account economic dimension (eg. job creation), social dimension (eg. resolution of a social need for a vulnerable group) and environmental dimension (eg. reduction of impact on the environment). Table 3 presents the results of this analysis

Table 3: Sustainability assessment of BVS projects (data results)

Project name	Public target	Social	Econ-omic	Environ-mental
"Centro ABCReal Portugal"	Autistic children and young people	x		
"Polo Social Manto"	Disadvantaged communities	x	x	
"Projeto Viver, Crescer e Integrar"	Immigrant population	x		
"Social Innovation Challenge"	Students (high school)	x		
"A Vida Vale"	The elderly	x		
"Agência ODM"	Students in higher	x		

Project name	Public target	Social	Economic	Environmental
	education			
"Audiodescrição.pt – ouço, logo vejo"	People with visual disabilities	x		
"Capital Aldeia"	Rural population of the village of Safara	x	x	
"Casa da Cidadania"	Different social groups	x		
"Centro de Interpretação da Abelha"	Beekeepers in the village of Terra Chã	x	x	
"Cidadania Plena"	Women immigrants - Brazil and African countries (portuguese language)	x	x	
"Cozinhar o Futuro"	Teenage mothers	x	x	
"Crescer Com Afetividade"	Marginalized youth	x		
"Crescer dos 8 aos 80"	Families from disadvantaged classes	x		
"EC3, Eco-Centro de Compostagem Caseira"	Children from kindergarten to secondary level	x		x
"Educação é a Melhor Prevenção"	Children, parents and grandparents	x		
"EfeitoD"	Patients with trisomy 21	x	x	
"Formar Campões para a Vida"	Children and youth at risk	x		
"Lar Telhadinho"	People with disabilities and their families	x		
"Lavandaria Solidária"	Vulnerable social groups	x	x	
"Mais Cuidados, Mais Integrados"	Ethnic minorities	x		
"Passos de Tempo"	The elderly	x		
"Piscina Terapêutica os 4 Elementos"	People with disabilities	x		

Project name	Public target	Social	Economic	Environmental
"Por ti" – Projecto de Apoio a ti	Families with low incomes	x		
"Porto de Abrigo"	Disadvantaged youth and adults from 16 years with intellectual development problems	x	x	
"Retalhos de Esperança"	Unemployed women	x	x	x
"Rir é o melhor remédio?"	Hospitalized children, families, health professionals	x		
"Saúde a Sorrir"	Disadvantaged, excluded or marginalized communities	x		
"Semear o Futuro"	People with hearing impairments and autism	x	x	
"Serviço de Intervenção e Apoio à Criança"	Children with disabilities	x		

Source: The Authors

The information about sustainability dimensions was organized, as shown in table 3, in a simplified way that provides a global perspective on the three dimensions assessed. The reason for this approach is related to the difficulty in collecting more objective indicators shared by all organizations, as well as in the divergence of these organizations, concerning their activity and the availability of public information. These difficulties, concerning the definition of finance and social measures, are referred to by several other authors (Austin et al., 2006). According to Young, (2006), an effort has been made in this direction through the development of mechanisms that can support the creation of new metrics in order to quantify value in the social sector; however this case study did not allow for the identification of different metrics.

Further to this subject, and in accordance with the classification presented in the literature review (Costa and Carvalho, 2011) the social organizations studied are include in the first group, i.e., social entrepreneurship refers to the initiatives of social organizations in search ofalternative financing strategies or as a way of creating social value through management practices (Dees, 1998a; Austin, Stevenson and Wei-Skiller, 2006; Boschee, 1998).

The analysis of table 3 indicates that the most relevant value created by these projects is social; nevertheless, some of them also indirectly create some economic value, particularly through job creation and service revenues. These findings concur with the literature review, that refers that social entrepreneur may produce private gain in the process of creating social value (Emerson and Twersky, 1996).

6.   Concluding remarks

This article consolidated the theoretical approach to the topics of social entrepreneurship. The work enabled the following considerations:

- The various organizations that constitute the social economy can contribute to the involvement of various actors and interest groups.
- The valuation of economic activity serving social needs, the more equitable distribution of income, job creation and wealth solidarity, and corrections of imbalances in the labor market are key factors for intervention in this area.
- This sector has started to have increasing importance because of increasing social needs unmet by the government.

Through the empirical study it could be seen that the attractiveness of a projects and its funding depends on factors which include the social entrepreneur's proactivity, the stakeholders' involvement, the age of the project, the region and the type of public target. We expected to find some patterns between these factors that could justify their attractiveness to possible investors, but that did not happen. However, it was possible to identify some common vectors concerning the four projects with 100% funding. It was therefore possible to conclude that the higher involvement of different stakeholders and sponsors, the linkage with reputable organizations which have a wide contact network and a history of success, historical and organizational seniority, entrepreneur proactivity and stakeholders participation are issues that are important for the project's attractiveness.

It was also possible to see that the social organizations involved do not have metrics to quantify the value created. The existence of such metrics could improve the performance of the organization. A more organized and transparent performance, through the availability of public information, could lead to better results and better recognition of their activity from the community, possible investors and other stakeholders.

We also conclude that the most relevant value created by these projects is social; some of them, however, also indirectly create some economic value, particularly through job creation and services revenues.

Finally this study presented a diversity of projects that demonstrate a strong creativity amongst social entrepreneurs, particularly in the fields of social cohesion and regional development, revealing that social entrepreneurship and its key players can definitely make a strong contribution to improving the welfare of populations.

7. Appendix 1: Interview guide

Main objectives	Specific objectives
Understand degree of project attractiveness	Project value
	Shares sold
	% Funding
Understand the reasons of project attractiveness	Initial date
	Region
	Scope of activities
	Type of organization
	Entrepreneur activity
	Stakeholders participation
	Public target
Assessment of project sustainability	Economic dimension
	Social dimension
	Environmental dimension

References

Aldrich, H.; Zimmer, C. (1986). Entrepreneurship through social networks. In D. Sexton & R. Smilor (Eds.), *The art and science of entrepreneurship,* New York: Ballinger, pp 3-23

Alvord, A. S., D. Brown e C. W. Letts (2002), "Social Entrepreneurship and Social Transformation: An Exploratory Study", *Hauser Center for Nonprofit Organizations: The Kennedy School of Government*, Harvard University.

Alvord, S. H., Brown, L. D., e Letts, C. W. (2004), "Social entrepreneurship and societal transformation", *Journal of Applied Behavioral Science*, 40(3), pp 260–282.

Austin, J., Stevenson, H., Wei-Skillern, J. (2006). "Social and commercial entrepreneurship: Same, different, or both?" *Entrepreneurship Theory and Practice*, 30(1), 1–22

Birley, S. (1985). "The role of networks in the entrepreneurial process". *Journal of Business Venturing*, 1, pp 107–117.

Bolsa de Valores Sociais disponível em
http://www.bvs.org.pt/view/viewPrincipal.php

Boschee, J. (1998), "Merging mission and money: A board member's guide to social entrepreneurship", disponível em:
http://www.socialent.org/pdfs/MergingMission.pdf, 20 October 2010.

Costa, Teresa, Carvalho, Luísa (2011), "Empreendorismo social: estado de arte", *Revista Gestin*, forthcoming.

Dees, J.G. (2001). The meaning of "social entrepreneurship". Available at http://www.fuqua.duke.edu/ centers/case/documents/dees_SE.pdf

Dees, J.G. (2007). "Taking social entrepreneurship seriously" *Society*, 44(3), pp 24–31.

Domenico, L.; Haugh, H.; Tracey, P. (2010) "Social Bricolage: Theorizing social value creation in social enterprises" Entrepreneurship Theory and practice, 681-703

Dorado, S. (2006). "Social entrepreneurial ventures: Different values so different processes of creation, no?" *Journal of Developmental Entrepreneurship*, 11(4), pp 319–343.

Emerson, J. and Twersky, F. (eds), (1996), New social entrepreneurs: the success, challenge and lessons of non-profit enterprise creation, San Francisco: Roberts Foundation, Homeless Economic Development Fund.

Hockerts, K. (2006). Entrepreneurial opportunity in social purpose ventures. In J. Mair, J. Robinson, & K. Hockerts (Eds.), *Social entrepreneurship*. London: Palgrave, 142-154

Johannisson, B. (2000). Networking and entrepreneurial growth. In D. Sexton & H. Landstrom (Eds.), *Handbook of entrepreneurship,* , London: Blackwell, 368–386

King, P. J., e Roberts, N. C. (1987), "Policy entrepreneurs: Catalysts for policy innovation", *Journal of State Government*, 60, pp 172–178.

Leadbeater, C. (2007), "Social enterprise and social innovation: Strategies for the next ten years", CabinetOffice, Office of the Third Sector, November 2007, available at
http://www.charlesleadbeater.net/cms/xstandard/social_enterprise_innovation.pdf

Lewis, E. (1980). Public entrepreneurship: Toward a theory of bureaucratic power. Bloomington, IN: Indiana University Press.

Mair, J. (2006). Introduction to part II: Exploring the intentions and opportunities behind social entrepreneurship. In J. Mair, J. Robinson, & K. Hockerts (Eds.), *Social entrepreneurship*. New York: Palgrave Macmillan, 89-94

Mair, J.; Marti, I. (2006). "Social entrepreneurship research: A source of explanation, prediction, and delight". *Journal of World Business*, *41*, pp 36–44.

Mulgan, G.; Tucker, S.;Sli, R.; Sanders, B. (2007), "Social innovation - what it is, why it matters and how it can be accelerated", The Young Foundation: Oxford available at
http://www.sbs.ox.ac.uk/centres/skoll/research/Documents/Social%20Innovation.pdf.

Neck, H.; Brush, C. Allen, E. (2009) "The landscape of social entrepreneurship" *Business Horizons*, 52, 1, pp 3-19

Peredo and McLean, (2006), Social entrepreneurship: A critical review of the concept, *Journal of World Business* 41 (1), pp 56–65.

Phills Jr, James, Deiglmeier, Kriss and Miller, Dale T. (2008), "Rediscovering Social Innovation," Stanford Social Innovation Review", *6*(4), 34.

Robinson, J. (2006). Navigating social and institutional barriers to markets: How social entrepreneurs identify and evaluate opportunities. In J. Mair, J. Robinson, & K. Hockerts (Eds.), *Social entrepreneurship*. New York: Palgrave Macmillan, pp 95-120

Sagawa, S and Segal, E. (2000), Common interest, common good: creating value through business and social sector partnerships, Boston, MA: Harvard Business and Social Sector Partnership.

Seelos, C. and Mair, J. (2005), "Entrepreneurs in service of the poor – models for business contributions to sustainable development", *Business Horizons*, Vol. 48 No. 3,,pp 241-6.

Shaw and Carter, 2007 E. Shaw and S. Carter, Social entrepreneurship: Theoretical antecedents and empirical analysis of entrepreneurial processes and outcomes, *Journal of Small Business and Enterprise Development* 14 (3) (2007), pp 418–434.

Thompson, J. (2002). "The world of the social entrepreneur". *International Journal of Public Sector Management*, *15*(5), pp 412–431.

Venkataramann, S. (1997), The distinctive domain of entrepreneurship research: An editors perspective, J. Katz & R. Brockhaus (Eds) *Advances in Entrepreneurship firm emergence and growth*, 3, pp 119-138, JAI Press.

Waddock, S. A. (1988), "Building successful social partnerships", *Sloan Management Review* 29(4), pp 17-22.

Yin, R.. (1994). *Case Study Research. Design and Methods,* London, Sage Publications.

Young, R. (2006), For what it is worth: Social value and the future of social entrepreneurship. In: A. Nicholls, Editor, *Social entrepreneurship: New models of sustainable social change*, Oxford University Press, Oxford, UK (2006), pp 56–73.

www.ingramcontent.com/pod-product-compliance
Lightning Source LLC
Chambersburg PA
CBHW050529270326
41926CB00015B/3132